Praise for *Value Creation*

"Businesses know a lot more about IT today, and they demand the IT organization know more about business. This book provides answers to the provocative question of how the CIO can become a true partner to the executives who run the business."

—Rob Simplot
President and CEO, RCG Global Services

"This book brings a fresh insight and understanding of the complex relationships between business success and technological advances. This framework provides a great way to use new and current technology and to integrate with the processes and culture of the company."

—Bill Seibel
CEO, Mobiquity

"Excellent insight! This book, based on a great deal of practical experience, boils down a very complex topic into an understandable and common sense approach. In addition to a holistic approach to capture how IT enables businesses, Bhatia has highlighted the human element that is key to running a business and bringing all these concepts in perfect harmony."

—Mark Sohl
COO, Generation Mortgage

"Today's CIO must be an intrinsic part of the business to really enable strategies, and this book provides a great structure to think of both effectiveness and efficiency. It will help any business executive to focus the IT debate on creating business value and ultimately shift the thinking from 'utility' to 'value creation.'"

—Sandra Hofmann
CIO-in-Residence, Advanced Technology Development Center

"An excellent work for putting together the Information Technology value proposition in a present day context. A must-read for all executives and business people to understand how to leverage IT and knit it into the fabric of their business processes properly."

—Mark Perlstein
President and CEO, DatAvail

"I recommend *Value Creation* to any executive in the public or private sector to see how they can operationalize their strategies for revenue growth or operation excellence. A practical guide and an eye-opener to viewing your processes and systems."

—Cindy Tierney
CIO, Beazer Homes

"If you are in a business and wonder how technology is changing the way the work is done and why, *read this book*. This captures business process thinking and how technologies prevalent today affect business results."

—Peter Gordon
SVP, Enterprise Strategy, Fidelity National Information Services

"The business has to acknowledge that IT is a fundamental enabler to the business growth strategy. In order to do so, there must be an acceptance not only of IT growth opportunities, but of the amount of 'maintenance' investments. Bhatia captures this in a succinct and crisp fashion in his book. The crux is to see how to balance investments and risks to increase shareholder value."

—Vicki Hamilton
SVP, Enterprise Digital Operations, Turner Broadcasting

"'IT happens', and we all need to be cognizant of it and understand the pros and cons of thinking through all of it up-front. Bhatia has done an excellent job of educating the reader, IT executive, IT user, hiring manager of IT resources in corporations, etc. by leveling the playing field in clarifying the true value to business. This book is a great investment and I encourage the audience to give it serious consideration, as it would directly impact their and their organization's success in the second decade of this millennium."

—Dr. Shree Nanguneri
President and CEO, MGBS, Inc.

VALUE
CREATION

VALUE
CREATION

Linking Information Technology
and Business Strategy

ASHU BHATIA

Brown Books Publishing Group
Dallas, Texas

Value Creation
Linking Information Technology and Business Strategy

Brown Books Publishing Group
16250 Knoll Trail, Suite 205
Dallas, Texas 75248
www.brownbooks.com
(972) 381-0009

ISBN 978-1-61254-036-8
Library of Congress Control Number 2012930280

Printed in the United States of America
10 9 8 7 6 5 4 3 2 1

For more information, please visit www.AshuBhatia.com.

This book is dedicated to my father, who always tried to ignite in me the curiosity that keeps the candle of knowledge lit in all of us.

CONTENTS

AUTHOR'S NOTE

These are not times for careless spending in any area of a business. Unfortunately, while everyone agrees businesses must cut careless spending, the problem is defining "careless." Too often, executives want to make cuts in exactly the kinds of programs and projects that realize greater profitability—they save 2 percent by cutting something that saves (or profits) the company 10 percent. It's two steps forward and four back. We all see this happening in many places. In the current global economic climate, companies are trying to run off the extra fat. Across corporate America and other economies, the business news clearly details that productivity is at an all-time high, employees are working more, and laid-off workers have not been replaced. Liposuction may be good, but only to a point. This kind of economic climate also hovers over Information Technology (IT) organizations and their budgets, which are being squeezed even as IT roles are being switched to "keep the lights on" roles that focus on operations instead of innovation. Several IT initiatives are becoming focused on the bottom line rather than innovative top-line growth. It's all about reducing technology costs, managing enterprise risks, reducing enterprise-wide business costs, and so on. Many executives (CIOs, CFOs, and even COOs) are looking at optimizing their IT asset portfolio, and the questions they are asking are misguided. They ask:

- Is the IT organization really doing what the business wants from a corporate and business unit strategy perspective? Are we doing the right things?
- How can I reduce costs and inefficiencies in my IT operations? How can I reduce complexity within the IT environment? How can I do those things correctly?
- And lastly, if I am able to achieve the above-mentioned goals, how can I ensure that the chaos, once under control, does not return? Once I gain some IT portfolio health, how do I stay healthy over the long run?

The typical problem IT organizations face is that their IT spending level is usually based on historical or competitive benchmark levels, which is a lagging metric (more like driving by only looking into the rearview mirror) instead of a forward-looking metric (leading indicators, such as where growth will be, what capabilities we will need, etc.). Consequently, there is often a lack of recognition for IT's contribution to the business top line or bottom line. Compounding this problem, IT cost-cutting further drives down the value-adding and innovative IT initiatives. As a result, IT capabilities deteriorate and midterm IT operating costs rise.

This leads to a vicious circle that begins with business executives who do not understand the real need for IT strategic planning. The business dictates a solution, IT accepts it, and then IT resources are consumed by the complexity of a nonoptimal solution. There is pressure to deliver and consequently a high failure rate, rework rate, and, hence, low confidence in IT. This leads to a further breakdown in IT business relationships and fuels more misaligned initiatives from an IT perspective. This misaligned spiral just tends to get bigger with time and worsening economic cycles. At the end of the day, it's like tying a runner's legs together, loading him with weights, and then berating him for running too slowly. One imagines the whole approach could be best summed up by the corporate declaration, "The beatings will continue until morale improves."

Depending on the industry and company size, the key is surely to focus on costs and optimize the IT spend. But some structured thinking is needed to decide the difference between what should be discretionary IT spend and what is truly nondiscretionary IT spend. This book delves into the relationship of business value and Information Systems and will help you define a framework for your company, specific to your industry and your position within that industry, to achieve both effectiveness and efficiency in the IT organization. If that sounds like a big promise, it is. Somewhere in the past, some business forefathers looked at employees and decided that on the general ledger that item needs to be listed as a cost. It was only in the late twentieth and early twenty-first centuries that we reexamined this axiom, finally learning that employees were investments and, more importantly, assets to be groomed and nurtured as such to increase the return they bring. Now it's time to turn that same eye toward IT so that we increase returns far in excess of the savings we would get from simply cutting IT to the bone. Thus, the goal of this book is to show what value really is and then show how IT can target value to enhance this objective rather than detract from it. Since you took the time to look at this book, this book will help you:

> Thus, the goal of this book is to show what value really is and then show how IT can target value to enhance this objective rather than detract from it.

- Focus the IT debate on creating business value—Using relevant metrics and recognized diagnostic tools, this book will help shift the IT debate from "utility" to "value creation."

- Optimize the IT investment agenda—Are we investing the right amount? Have we targeted and prioritized the right opportunities to pursue? Are we executing most effectively? Is the IT budget really strategy-aligned and business case–supported to maximize ROI and create a strategic advantage?
- Transform your IT organization and capabilities therein— Have we industrialized key operational processes? Are we achieving necessary business service levels?

ONE

Introduction

What's the use of running if you are not on the right road?
—Unknown

The real issue of business and IT alignment and integration arises from a true understanding of the company's business imperatives across the entire enterprise. Business imperatives define the outcomes that the business must achieve in order to support its corporate strategies. They are direct, actionable statements with measurable targets. Business imperatives should provide direction for all key business decisions. As Robert H. Miles said in his book *Leading Corporate Transformation*, "Successful corporate transformations do not spring from energy alone. That energy must be focused on a clear, concise, and compelling vision of a highly desirable future state." Clear business imperatives should quantify key priorities for the business in the short- and long-term future and should be collected through business interviews with key stakeholders and leadership within the business. People often ask how to differentiate the business imperatives from business nice-to-haves. Well, if the price of the status quo is more than the cost of transformation, it becomes a business imperative—a burning platform. This is elaborated by the true story of a survivor of a fire on an oil rig. One of the workers at the rig jumped eleven stories into freezing water because the deck was on fire. When interviewed later and asked how he managed to jump, his response was, "It was a choice between imminent death and some probability of survival."

What is Business Value?

Alice: Would you tell me, please, which way I ought to go from
*   here?*
The Cat: That depends a good deal on where you want to get to.
Alice: I don't much care where . . .
The Cat: Then it doesn't much matter which way you go.
Alice: . . . so long as I get somewhere.
The Cat: Oh, you're sure to do that, if only you walk long enough.
        —Lewis Carroll, *Alice in Wonderland*

If you think about the trends and new forces that are reshaping most industries and almost all businesses today, you have to break them all down to the basics of what is happening.

There is a shift to a multipolar world. The world was "flat" long before Tom Friedman wrote the book (*The World is Flat*). Mergers and acquisitions, along with the expansion of global companies, have led to the global management of assets. Most medium- to large-scale companies have to manage global thought capital as well as other global assets spread all around the world. Also, the emergence of major regional and global companies from the BRIC countries (Brazil, Russia, India, and China) has led to newfound competition. The companies today are so networked in global assets and global economies that it's tough to look at them in a single country or continent anymore. As Martin Luther King Jr. said, "We are tied together in the single garment of destiny, caught in an inescapable network of mutuality."

Secondly, there is a separation and dislocation of production and consumption. Consider the breakup of the value chain into areas where the non-core competencies are not only outsourced but also drive a need for homogenization and industrialization of many areas of the value chain.

With the dynamic changes in global assets and workforce, companies need to look at dis-aggregating the value chain components of their business, re-source on an as-needed basis, mix alliances, and the like. Companies constantly need to be looking at strategies to enable value chain collaboration and strategies that optimize workforce productivity. Companies across the world are looking at these kinds of options, which focus only on their core strengths. Penske Truck Leasing outsources dozens of business processes to Mexico and India, and it cites greater efficiency and customer service as its reasons. In 2005, Wachovia inked a $1.1 billion deal with India's Genpact to outsource finance and accounting jobs and its human resources programs to Hewitt Associates. Of the $600 million to $1 billion Wachovia hopes to take out in costs over three years, it reinvested up to 40 percent into branches, ATMs, and personnel to boost its core business. In fact, a statement by the CEO of one of the niche outsourcing firms was this: "Many CEOs are saying, 'Don't tell me how much I can save. Show me how we can grow by 40 percent without increasing our capacity in our non-core business areas.'"

Along with this, consolidation for scale has always been a goal followed by companies ever since Adam Smith identified and promoted the value of specialization and mass production, which stated the universal economic law that a producer's average cost per unit falls as the scale of output is increased. The classic example, taken from Smith's book *Wealth of Nations*, is that of a pin factory in which ten men, each carrying out one or two of the eighteen operations needed to make a pin, are able to produce forty-eight thousand pins in a single day, while working separately they would be unable to make even two hundred pins in a day.

Finally, we also need to look at the "uber shift" toward self service and the opportunities this offers. Companies at the forefront of this shift are almost "outsourcing to their customers." What this means is that more and more companies are shifting work and choice to the customer. This has led to the redesign of front-end architecture and replacement of core systems by next generation systems. Companies today need to resemble a "handmade shoe" in that services and products are to be customized and nonreplicable. This makes it expensive to integrate new businesses into the organization.

Companies have to start thinking of business value as:

- *Differentiation* "on the outside"—They need to have a clear view of what makes them unique—product, sales, service, brand, or business model. They need to deliver a consistently positive experience for customers in each market segment.
- *Simplification* "on the inside"—They need simplicity in everything they do, and this means standardized or componentized internal products, processes, and systems, with scalable and repeatable business models across the enterprise.
- *Execution* mastery—They need to prioritize execution as a core capability with the right leadership skills, culture, and change and risk management.

With such trends it is important to know what Business Value is, what its historical context has been, and how it might be tapped in the times to come. This is a big proposition, but you can only eat an elephant one bite at a time. So before we start thinking of "Business Value" from a company's point of view, it is important to establish the concept from an individual's point of view.

Consider: Whenever you intend to purchase something from a marketplace, you think about the value for your money. If you are buying a car, you think of value from your perspective. You think of hard variables like mileage per gallon of fuel, maintenance cost during its lifetime, and so on. You also think of soft variables like prestige, brand image, the cool factor, or the practicality factor. Of course, there are other considerations that are important to you—security, emissions, and even practicality of servicing. So what is value? Is it worth the price of the car or the monthly payments you need to make?

That thought process builds into the economic forefront of businesses as well, whether you utilize IT as a cost center or profit center, or whether you consider capital expenses for investment or cloud computing solutions (like a recurring lease payment without an up-front price for my car). In any case, you need to understand what you are getting and what you are giving. To help build this understanding, it is important to understand the evolution of the term *business value* over the decades.

In the 1960s, it was all about maximizing market share, because the industrial revolution ensured that if the fixed costs of a company were spread across more volumes, business value was enhanced. In the 1980s, the focus shifted to profitability and metrics like return on equity or return on assets, focusing on accounting logic. The last couple of decades distilled the idea to a financial logic, and industry gurus began to say that business value is all about financial returns to the shareholders—whether it's share price, dividends, or measurements like economic value added (EVA) or market value added (MVA). But at a basic level the value of the firm reflects the expectations of shareholders regarding future cash generation:

> The value of the firm reflects the expectations of shareholders regarding future cash generation.

- *Financial return*—How much cash will the company generate? How much cash injection will it need?
- *Risk*—How certain is the cash generation and realization of the investment (capital gain)?
- *Time*—When will cash be generated? When will value be harvested?

Of course, review of historical value creation is a key element to predicting future value creation. Research has shown that cash-based approaches are effective shareholder evaluation methods. However, people know that more and more businesses today are people-centric in terms of assets, and that means employee productivity is as important as capital productivity. Still, by focusing on cash, combining operating and capital expenditure, and taking into account the risks of the business, shareholder value analysis (SVA) provides a single measure to evaluate business performances. SVA can be used both to review historical performance and to assess potential future value creation.

> Shareholder value analysis (SVA) can be used both to review historical performance and to assess potential future value creation.

With regard to *historic* value creation, SVA provides a historical perspective on sources of value creation and value destruction (the value of business units, customer groups, and products). It also identifies which operational value drivers need to be impacted in order to enhance value creation. This helps identify how individual firms perform against them.

Taking into consideration *future* value creation, such a framework establishes a clear link between strategy and the impact on operational levers; it further helps in modeling changes in shareholder value. It helps the executive teams determine how changes in the industry might impact value creation. It also builds a model that can help review individual investment decisions.

According to the value based management approach, the focus of planning and control systems is on creating value for shareholders through actions aimed at optimizing the risk–return profile for shareholders. As shown in the following figure, the advocates of SVA determined the components of true value. It is simply created by:

7

1. Increasing profit/margin, which is achieved by increasing revenue and decreasing costs. Revenue is dependent on the product/service volumes, mix, and their prices. Costs that go into a product/service are cost of goods sold (COGS), sales, general administrative (SGA) costs, advertising, etc.

2. Reducing the capital deployed into the business, which is done by optimizing the fixed assets and reducing the working capital.

Figure 1: Shareholder Value Tree

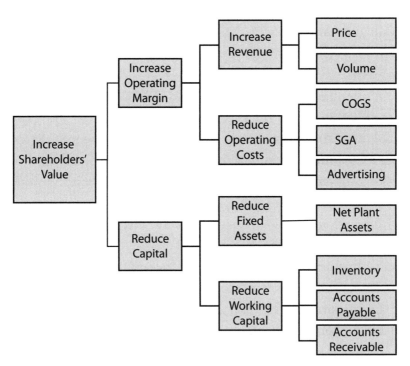

This value creation framework—again, just like the considerations that go into your own decision on buying a car—is useful in understanding how different financial indicators drive a company's intrinsic value through their impact on cash flows to the company.

Ultimately, we want to understand what is driving the company's value creation. You can think of it more easily when you break it down into components.

> Value is created when spread, the difference between return on invested capital (ROIC) and weighted average cost of capital (WACC), is increased.

1. Value is created when **spread**, the difference between return on invested capital (ROIC) and weighted average cost of capital (WACC), is increased. It's similar to the way a household will have more cash when the income exceeds the costs of living.

2. ROIC is made up of two components: the operating margin, which is the ratio of EBITA (earnings before interest, taxes, and amortization) and revenue (EBITA/revenue). EBITA is defined as the earnings before the deduction of interest, tax, and amortization. The operating margin measures how effectively the company converts revenue into profits.

3. The other component is capital turnover, which is the ratio of revenues to invested capital (revenues/invested capital). This measures how effectively the company employs its invested capital.

As shown in the following figure, the operating margin ratios can be decomposed into COGS, SGA, and depreciation. The capital turnover can be decomposed into utilization of working capital, property, plant, and equipment (PPE), and other assets.

Figure 2: ROIC Tree

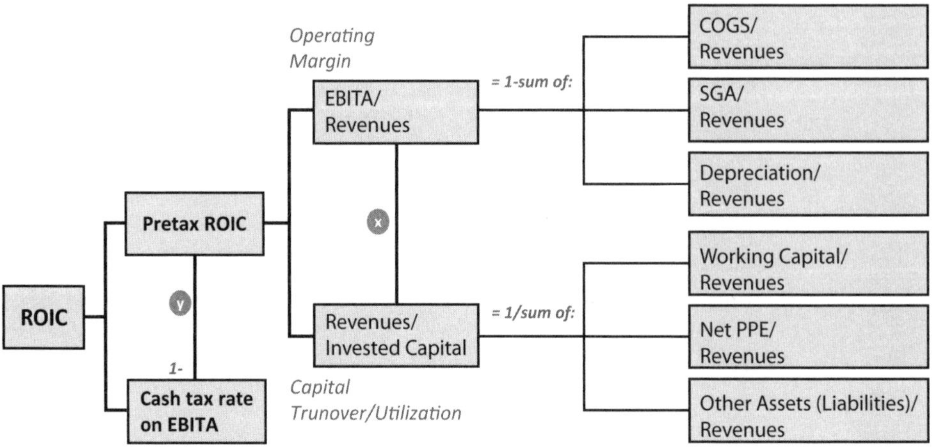

ROIC: Retun on Invested Capital
EBITA: Earnings before Interest, Taxes, and Amortization
SGA: Selling, General, and Administrative
PPE: Prperty, Plant, and Equipment

Value is also created when positive spread is "magnified" through growth in cash flow through pure greenfield innovation (e.g., at companies such as Apple, Google, etc.) or mergers and acquisitions (e.g., banks, Telcos, etc.). As shown in the following bullets, *spread* is the difference of rate of return on the money you invest and the cost rate for that money. Even in a simple business everyone knows they need to make more than the bank charges them for interest. If you borrow money at 4 percent and are making a return of 15 percent, then your spread is 11 percent. As explained in the book *Blue Ocean Strategy* by W. Chan Kim and Renée Mauborgne, another component of value creation— *Growth*—is an outcome of having innovative products/services that create a great demand with customers. This can be done by the company itself or sometimes through strategic mergers and acquisitions.

Figure 3: Value Creation Through Spread and Growth

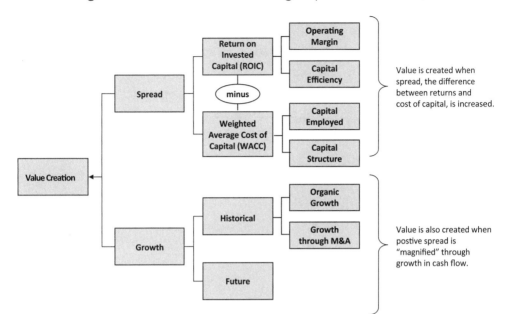

Thus, the business strategy then becomes management of strategic options for growth. A strategic option is one that makes a specific and fundamental change to the business's value proposition, to its value network, and/or to its revenue model. The options for reinvigorating value become transformation, greenfield, and mergers and acquisitions.

Businesses and academics began focusing on measuring value as SVA quite some time ago. In 1919, the Michigan Supreme Court ruled, in *Dodge vs. Ford Motor Company,* in favor of shareholder primacy, stating that "[a] business corporation is organized and carried on primarily for the benefit of the stockholders. The powers of the directors are to be employed for that end." Henry Ford and company directors had decided *not* to pay a dividend, despite substantial retained earnings that year, so that the money could be spent on plant expansion. The court ruled that this reason was not directed at the profit of the company and therefore was not a basis for refusal to pay a dividend. Since then shareholder value has become the mantra of corporate functions. But because of the interdependence and linkages of complete business value chains with customers, employees, partners, the community, and so on, there was a clear indication that for a holistic approach to measuring value you need to consider multiple elements. A holistic view of business value takes into account not only shareholders, but also customers (quality, service, etc.), employees (commitment), business partners (innovation, synergies, etc.), and the community (social responsibility, goodwill, etc.).

In a free enterprise, a corporation has direct responsibility to a lot of stakeholders. As Arie de Geus said at the European Business Forum,

> Businesses are still governed by antiquated corporation laws. In the past, employees were regarded as an adjunct to business; they were simply the "hands" to operate the machines. Power was concentrated at the top. The law gave priority to the shareholders, based on the assumption that the human elements were mere extensions of the capital assets. Most of today's corporations, however, have fewer capital assets. They are dependent on brain power; people are the critical success factor. But businesses are still ruled by nineteenth-century legislation. Managers are forced to optimize capital before all other concerns. Excessive power is given to shareholders and that power is being abused.

> Wise decision makers in business look at the long-term impact today's choices will have tomorrow—on people, on the community, and on the opinions of customers.

Smart business decisions are not just a matter of counting up short-term dollars and cents. Wise decision makers in business look at the long-term impact today's choices will have tomorrow—on people, on the community, and on the opinions of customers. Especially in recent years, many consumers have been upset by widely publicized examples of fraud by companies and executives. As a result, consumers have become more conscious of whom they are doing business with and which products they should buy. Many companies that are seeking for long-term profitability are looking for ways to become more socially responsible. Striving for social responsibility helps individuals, organizations, and governments have a positive impact on business and society, which enables a positive contribution to bottom-line results. One of the best quotes for this corporate balancing acts was by Saj-nicole Joni and Ken Favaro in the magazine *strategy+business* (May 2011):

> Every business faces the opposing forces of the pull for more growth against the pull for more profitability; the demand to show profit today against the need to invest in the company's future; and the call for optimizing the whole against the tendency of individual parts to maximize their own performance. The three performance tensions—growth versus profitability, short term versus long term, and whole versus parts—provide fundamental energy that can be harnessed to deliver superior, sustainable results. The ability of the board, CEO, and executive team to navigate these tensions largely determines their company's ability to both create wealth and serve society.

Value of IT

If everyone is thinking alike, someone isn't thinking.
This is a strategy session!

—Peter Drucker, management consultant and author,
coined the term "knowledge worker"

Now that we understand the concept of business value, the real question is how IT enables business value for a company. If you ask this question of business executives, you'd be amazed at the variety of responses. The CEO is focused on shareholder value and direction setting. The questions in his or her mind are: How can I better use IT to deliver shareholder value? How can I use IT to better focus on our business strategy? Am I spending the right amount on IT?

The COO is focused on business operations effectiveness and efficiency. The questions in his or her mind are: How can IT reduce my costs of operation? Are there better ways to use technology to become more effective? How can I deliver more value to every part of my business?

The CFO is focused on return on investments, controls, and governance. The questions in his or her mind are: What is the true cost structure of my IT organization? How should IT costs be allocated among the businesses? How can we get a return on our invested IT capital? How do I measure the value and results from IT?

So every stakeholder thinks of a business initiative from his or her point of view. It reminds one of the story of Alexander the Great. After Alexander had conquered Egypt, King Darius of Persia offered Alexander generous terms for peace. Darius would pay Alexander ten thousand talents for releasing Persian prisoners, give him the areas west of the Euphrates, and hand over his daughter to

Alexander in marriage. Alexander was unsure if he should accept these terms and consulted his general, Parmenion. Parmenion said, "If I were Alexander, I would accept these offers." Alexander countered, "So would I, if I were Parmenion."

The CIO working within a company has the advantage of being able to look at the operations, finance, marketing, etc., since he or she is providing services to every business area. This person should think of the value for the enterprise as a whole. C. K. Prahalad said in the magazine *Optimize,*

> The CIO needs to be focused on IT Value and running the IT operations efficiently. The questions in his/her mind are: How can I align IT with the business drivers, and what technologies should we invest in? How can I improve service and balance, meeting all needs while managing costs? What information needs to be integrated to deliver value? How do we keep the multitude of technologies integrated? Who should I involve in decision making? CIOs should ask themselves two questions: "How well can we convert business ideas into business processes?" and "How flexible are my systems to translate BP into IT?" Those who make this transition will be the facilitators of their companies' success. If not, they will be the bottleneck. The choice is clear: CIOs must be the bridge in the logic chain between strategy and operational excellence.

The interests of business and technology can quickly diverge unless they are linked correctly with effective metrics. And with such a spectrum of concerns, it's no wonder that every few years, it seems, the role of the CIO becomes an agenda issue. Should it be reinvented? Should it survive? Sometimes the attention is sparked by the subpar performance of corporate IT functions. More often, the closer scrutiny is linked directly to the information technology itself and the new threats and opportunities it presents to business.

Ever since the *Harvard Business Review* article by Nicholas G. Carr—"IT Doesn't Matter"—came out in May 2003, there has been debate on the topic, and this debate gathers more fire with the waxing and waning of the global and domestic economy. Nicholas Carr wrote,

> I examine the evolution of information technology in business and show that it follows a pattern strikingly similar to that of earlier technologies like railroads and electric power. For a brief period, as they are being built into the infrastructure of commerce, these "infrastructural technologies," as I call them, open opportunities for forward-looking companies to gain strong competitive advantages. But as their availability increases and their cost decreases—as they become ubiquitous—they become commodity inputs. From a strategic standpoint, they become invisible; they no longer matter.

But the key is that IT can still be leveraged as an innovative enabler and will be as long as IT management does create competitive advantage with all other things kept constant.

People generally ask, "Should the CIO report to the CEO or the CFO?" In my experience, many CIOs in 2010 were let go and have not been replaced. This shows that IT was being used in a utility model at those places anyway. If the CIO is not reporting to the CEO, IT is not considered a strategic enabler. This book goes into areas where IT can perform value targeting and finally enable and deliver value creation. Significant opportunities exist for CIOs to influence the business agenda in a material way and add value beyond the adoption of leading fundamentals. These opportunities should be considered in light of individual company strategy and overall industry dynamics. Suggested influences to consider in shaping IT strategy include:

- Your company-specific profit drivers and value structure (the primary types of assets that drive value, such as intellectual property or physical assets).
- The level of change within your industry.
- Influences of competition at all levels of the value chain.

If there's any issue that routinely frustrates executives in many organizations, it's how to get a true fix on the value that IT adds to the businesses it serves. IT is undoubtedly central to creating value and therefore continues to account for a rising share of total investment. But defining, measuring, and maximizing that value remain elusive. The imperfect relationship between business managers and their IT counterparts is a long-standing problem, and in a lot of industries you will find that IT isn't a core competency. It's more or less a support function—running data centers or preparing and servicing different clients. Hence, management unfortunately views IT as a cost center. The fact is that if you compare 2010 to, say, twenty years ago, businesses know a lot more about IT, and they expect the IT organization to know more about the business. There is always the debate surrounding the CIO trying to have a seat at the decision-making process during strategic planning, as well as a lot of debate about whether (and how) the IT organization can become a true partner. In my experience, as the enterprises mature, the CIO function is becoming the center of all corporate functions of the entire organization. He or she is interacting with finance, sales and marketing, operations, HR, etc. The CIO is in a position to really help the CMO with campaign management and lead generation, help the CFO with cost optimization and measurement, help the COO with utilization metrics and supply chain visibility, and so on. So

> The CIO function can truly be the hub of the typical hub-and-spoke model.

if the CIO is truly a change agent, he or she can really influence the organization by providing a complete perspective to each functional area when at times these functions act in silos. The CIO function can truly be the hub of the typical hub-and-spoke model.

The hub-and-spoke model—centered around a similar concept to the hub and spokes on a wheel—was first pioneered by Delta Airlines in 1955, when Delta began scheduling airplanes to bring passengers to a hub airport where travelers would then connect to other Delta flights. This system would revolutionize air travel and business models in other fields, and its successful implementation revolves around the smooth, effective operation of the hub—the critical center of the process. Similarly, progressive CIOs are repositioning themselves and their IT organizations from being viewed as "service providers" to becoming "business value creators." By 2010, approximately 40 percent of CIOs were reporting directly to the CEO, which represented a measurable increase over the previous five years. This trend is likely to continue, creating new opportunities for CIO collaboration and competition with other C-suite executives to continuously find new sources of technology-enabled business value. CIOs can also create business value in new ways by enabling and maximizing new value propositions through enterprise integration, reducing enterprise-wide business costs, developing technology-based growth strategies, unlocking revenue potential of intellectual property, etc. This business value can come from unexpected places, as with the true story of Ludwig Roselius, a German coffee importer who discovered decaffeinated coffee in 1903. He tested a seawater-damaged shipment and noted most of the caffeine was gone from the beans, then had his team try to duplicate the result with technology. Three years later he launched decaffeinated coffee and named his new product Sanka, derived from the French "sans caffeine," meaning "without caffeine."

The way the CIO is typically polarized toward an area of the organization is dependent on the corporate strategy of the company.

If the company is focused on operational excellence, the work involves aligning to the metrics of the CFO and COO. If the strategy is customer intimacy, the CIO will be working very closely with the CMO. And if the company is trying to play a differentiation strategy, then the CIO will play more of a CTO role, trying to build capabilities within an organization that is constantly seeking competitive advantage in its products or services.

In some traditional sense, IT organizations used to play the service provider role. Their functions consisted of evaluating and prioritizing development projects, managing programs or projects, maintaining IT infrastructure, managing application portfolios, negotiating service delivery arrangements, and managing vendors. But in the current times when there is a real need to look at the business top line as well as the bottom line, IT organizations are beginning to look at aligning business and IT to generate incremental value, reduce technology costs, manage enterprise risks, and maximize ROI through predictable delivery of business solutions. As economies around the world emerge from the current downturn, many executives understand that what follows probably won't be just another turn of the business cycle. They must promote a much closer alignment between IT and the business units by embracing new models that call for joint decision making. IT should be looking at enabling and maximizing new value propositions through enterprise integration, developing technology-based growth strategies, and trying to unlock the revenue potential of intellectual property. Even if the company is more into physical assets (e.g., utilities, distribution, transportation, contract manufacturing, etc.), in today's world they have built knowledge that they should try to leverage to generate more value. For example, FedEx helped many catalog companies and direct marketers like Land's End to optimize their call centers and package distribution. Companies like WalMart share their information with suppliers like P&G to manage inventory in a more real-time manner. Trends like these make it clear that IT leaders must join with their business counterparts to seek out and implement technology-based innovations that will give companies long-term competitive advantages.

Even with the talk of utility models for IT infrastructure (standardized, harmonized, and run as cost efficiently as possible) and commoditization of non-core business processes, there is increased specialization and decentralization within core business processes (bridging the gap between business and IT and seeking value-adding new investment opportunities) to support a higher degree of value creation. As depicted below, the stack of a company's capabilities has layers that can be commoditized—common processes like HR, finance, etc. and supporting applications. But the specific processes and systems that give the company a distinct competitive advantage always need to be looked at to sustain and reinvent to further that advantage. The commodity boundary is all about doing it more efficiently than competition, whereas the value creation layer is all about being creative and effective and redefining the marketplace.

Figure 4: Commoditization and Specialization of IT Services

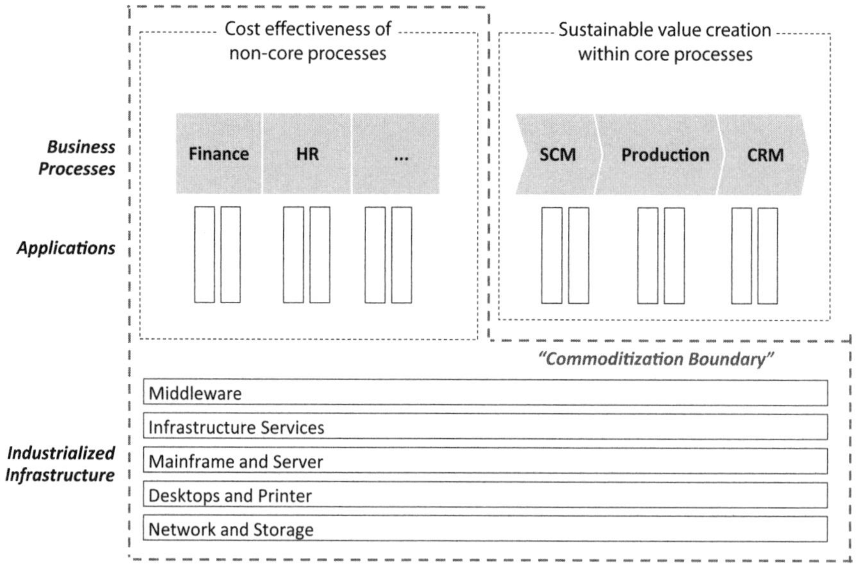

The mission of the IT organization is often expressed in terms of supporting or leading the business. "We will operate by aligning with our users' needs" or "IT will enable the business by . . ." are the mission statements by IT organizations. As a result, the creation of shareholder value is generally seen in **what** IT does for the business—new applications of technology. However, **how** IT is managed and delivers services can also drive shareholder value, resulting in a broader definition of benefits beyond cost reduction, a focus on the cost of capital, new operating models, better decision making, etc. Managing with an SVA perspective will improve IT's effectiveness as well as its efficiency.

Figure 5: Value of Information Technology

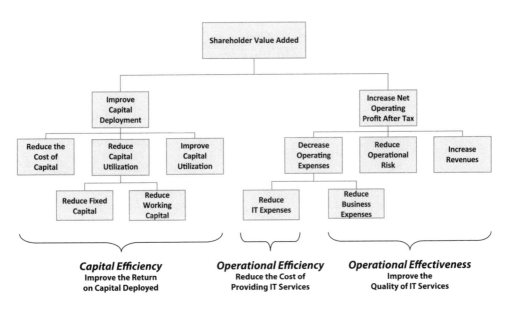

Capital Efficiency

There is always focus on reducing the level of fixed capital required to operate IT. The standardization and rationalization of the IT asset portfolio leads to reduction in capital charges. Standardization of IT assets also reduces working capital, since the use of re-sources for the maintenance of IT assets is reduced after the total IT asset footprint is brought under control. If the IT organization manages the risk and business continuity properly, it can influence operational stability and risk premium and thereby help reduce the cost of capital employed, specifically the cost of equity rate reduction. Finally, there is the issue of capital productivity. The IT organization can help improve the return on capital deployed by institutionalizing processes like improved application development productivity. It can also help generate revenues by leveraging assets to provide IT services to the external marketplace.

Examples in IT:

- The way IT organizations are looking to increase the company's capital efficiency is by developing sourcing strategies for activities that are capital intensive. There is a huge push to outsource technology infrastructure—data centers, network, etc.—as long as the information security risk is managed. Cloud computing options, as explained in chapter 3, are truly helping convert fixed costs to variable costs.

- With the advent of intellectual property in every industry, IT organizations can turn products into bundled services as well. GM selling OnStar services is an example of IT enabling a product transaction (typically the end of the customer touch point except for car servicing) to be turned into an ongoing service revenue stream. Many healthcare companies on the provider side have implemented revenue management systems because they have all the data flowing through their systems. As long as the privacy of patient information is not compromised, there are opportunities for IT-enabled revenue streams.

Operational Efficiency

For a couple of years now, CIOs have been decreasing IT expenses by reducing the cost of providing IT services.

Examples in IT:

- IT assets portfolio standardization and rationalization (as explained in chapter 5) through common platforms for applications and technology architecture (e.g., data centers, distributed computing, or networks) can immensely reduce the capex and opex allocation to such areas of the IT footprint.
- Mature IT organizations have developed vendor and alliance management capabilities and improved purchasing power by participating in a buying consortium.
- Since the consumer wants a lot of self-service capabilities anyway, IT organizations have extended those capabilities internally as well. This, along with leveraging emerging technologies to reduce expenses (such as mobile technology, network accessed storage, etc.), has helped bring some cost efficiencies to the IT organization budgets.
- Also, most IT organizations have been progressing over the years with the implementation of automation tools to provide end-to-end IT process improvements and methodologies for application development.

Operational Effectiveness

IT organizations can reduce business expenses by accelerating implementation of new solutions and reducing expenses through enhanced IT performance. An effective IT organization can also reduce the probability and impact of various operating risks, reduce the probability of revenue loss (e.g., trading floor down, online systems), improve customer attrition (e.g., due to poor service), and reduce reputation loss (e.g., the ability to attract new customers). All of these lead to operating expense reduction and creation of net new margin, as well as reduction of the cost of equity rate for the whole company. Finally, the IT organization can also accelerate the introduction of revenue-generating products and services and provide access to better customer relationship management (CRM) capabilities (as detailed in chapter 3) to create new top-line growth as well as enhanced margin.

Examples in IT:
- Some IT organizations have been operationally efficient in the manner they develop sourcing strategies for activities that require access to scarce skills and innovation (e.g., application development, new technologies, or new capabilities such as CRM data hosting and analysis). Many IT organizations also free up scarce resources to focus on higher value activities and outsource their legacy applications maintenance.
- Many IT organizations enhance business partner relationship management practices (as explained in chapter 3) through formal roles, responsibilities, processes, and tools. Also, broad usage of service level agreements (SLAs) or operating level agreements (OLAs) has enabled them to wring efficiencies from their suppliers.
- As IT organizations mature, especially from a federated model to a more shared services model (as detailed in chapter 3), they develop chargeback processes based on market rates as well as establish product/service catalogs to enable pricing transparency for business partners within the enterprise.
- With the current economic conditions, in which the focus on financial metrics for initiatives has pushed the whole company under the lens of the CFO, IT organizations are

implementing standard business case usage to establish the costs and benefits of their projects (as detailed in chapter 3).

TWO

Components of IT Strategy

Strategy without tactics is the slowest route to victory.
Tactics without strategy is the noise before defeat.

—Sun Tzu

The evolution of IT strategy has been dependent on economic conditions and the technology environment, as shown in the following table.

	Economic Condition	Technology Environment	IT Strategy
1970s	• Manufacturing recession	• Mainframe to mini-computers • Material resource planning systems	• Critical success factors • Very tactical focus
1980s	• Wall Street downturn • LBO environment • High interest rates	• Client–server computing • PC introduced	• Three-tiered architectures • Stages of growth

1990s	• Re-engineering hope for prolonged recession	• ERP applications • Unix serious business platform	• Front-end planning • Business case focus • E-commerce strategy
2000s	• Service recession	• Off-shore	• Very tactical focus • Driving to value and real metrics
2010+	• Global economic slowdown	• Utility computing • Mobility	• Reduce fixed assets • New channels of commerce

Easy as One, Two, Three

There are three components by which an IT organization can define its strategy—doing the right things, doing those things correctly, and maintaining the health of the IT asset portfolio. Depending upon the industry and company position, the organization will have to start with one area and get to other areas of focus. While a firm's IT strategy may map toward multiple areas, every organization will have a "dominant gene." That is to say, the organization, based upon the industry rate of change and the primary assets that drive value for the company, may have some immediate needs in doing the right things (alignment). And another company might need to first focus on internal IT processes

> There are three components by which an IT organization can define its strategy— doing the right things, doing those things correctly, and maintaining the health of the IT asset portfolio.

(doing the work correctly). So a key focus area will best define that organization's overall situation and serve as a good starting point to determine the highest priority opportunities for evaluation in value targeting. The three components of IT strategy are: (1) business and IT alignment, (2) integration of processes and tools to the IT systems, and (3) IT asset optimization.

Figure 6: Components of IT Strategy

IT Stategy (Demand Side and Supply Side)		
Business and IT Alignment	Integration of Processes and Tools	IT Asset Optimization
Do the right things	Do those things right	Get healthy and stay healthy

The first component, business and IT alignment, is about *effectiveness*. Doing the right things means that IT should take on initiatives that are truly aligned with business imperatives for the company. IT is undoubtedly central to creating value and therefore continues to account for a rising share of total investment. But defining, measuring, and maximizing that value remain elusive. And this discipline helps define the alignment and integration of IT with business. This is all about **WHAT** the IT organization should be doing. Chapter 3 will get into details of all the components of this section of a company's IT strategy.

The second component, alignment of processes and tools, is about *efficiency*—it is all about **HOW** the IT organization should be doing what it decides to take on. As the IT organizations have matured over the years, so have the processes and methodologies for execution of the initiatives—whether it's new capability development or just running the IT operations. Over the last couple of years, numerous software development methodologies have been introduced to guide development teams in achieving these quality goals. Some methodologies involve a disciplined and detailed process with strong emphasis on planning. Examples of such methods include the capability maturity model (CMM), the software process improvement and capability determination model (SPICE), team software process (TSP), etc. Then recently some *agile methods* have been advocated as a new paradigm for high-speed, quick-to-market software development. Examples include behavior driven development (BDD), extreme programming (XP), SCRUM, etc. The basic critique of the agile software development evangelists is that conventional software development processes are too rigid to achieve the end results, let alone the aimed quality factors for contemporary user-experience-driven projects. But one thing is for sure: no matter which process or methodology is applied, the bottom line is that there is an impact of software processes on the IT systems produced. Chapter 4 will get into details of all the components of this section of a company's IT strategy.

The third and last component, asset optimization, is about maintaining an optimized IT organization by managing your infrastructure and application portfolio—*get healthy and stay healthy*. Many years of distributed IS/IT spending and investment within specific functions and/or organization boundaries (no enterprise-wide investment management process) have resulted in redundant IT asset footprints in many organizations. Distributed computing has led to unchecked proliferation of under-utilized servers, and multiple systems often reside in different places and have different interfaces. Many organizations implemented or inherited applications at a furious pace during both the technology proliferation and merger and acquisition activity of the 1990s.

This fast growth in technology and ever-rising IT budgets quickly led to numerous and redundant applications in organizations. IT asset rationalization is the process of selecting the right set of strategic applications and infrastructure and then sunsetting or migrating the remaining set of IT assets to reduce the total footprint. Chapter 5 will get into details of all of the components of this section of a company's IT strategy—application rationalization, infrastructure, etc.

THREE

Do the Right Things

Only two kinds of person can catch a snake—one who is an expert and the other who does not know it's a snake.

—Unknown

I think the story about the little field mouse and the owl illustrates the importance of knowing what has to be done correctly before starting on the journey of execution. The mouse was lost in a dense wood, unable to find his way out. He came upon a wise old owl sitting in a tree. "Please help me, wise old owl—how can I get out of this wood?" said the field mouse. "Easy," said the owl. "Grow wings and fly out, as I do." "But how can I grow wings?" asked the mouse. The owl looked at him haughtily, sniffed disdainfully, and said, "Don't bother me with the details. I only decide the policy."

I guess it is clichéd to say in this day and age that IT needs to be aligned with business to deliver the right value for the organization. And there have been so many dissertations about how best to do that. Experts talk of how the role of the IT organization is changing from a service provider to that of a value creator.

Knowing what has to be built—in terms of capabilities for the company as a whole—is what keeps coherence between the services IT produces and the real needs of a company as a business. Without this knowledge, the story of five blind men is repeated across the company, in which every individual silo sees different strategic needs. According to the story, the blind men encounter an elephant and each man feeling a different part, concludes that the elephant, is like something else—a snake (the trunk), a brush (the hairy backside), a tree trunk (a leg), or a rope (the tail). Oftentimes, we have dramatically different perspectives of the very same thing because we only interact with one part of it. Knowledge of a company's needs as a whole is critical for each part of a successful IT organization.

The continuum starts with roles such as managing programs or projects, maintaining IT infrastructure, application portfolio rationalization, negotiating service delivery arrangements, etc.; it goes on to include the more strategic business focus of aligning business and IT to generate incremental value, reducing technology costs, managing enterprise risks, reducing enterprise-wide business costs, developing technology-based growth strategies, unlocking revenue potential of intellectual property, and the like.

> There is often a lack of recognition for IT's contribution to the business top line or bottom line.

The typical problem IT organizations face is that the IT spending level is usually based on historical or competitive benchmark levels. There is often a lack of recognition for IT's contribution to the business top line or bottom line. And IT cost cutting further drives down the value-adding and innovative IT initiatives. As a result, IT capabilities deteriorate and midterm IT operating costs rise. This leads to the vicious circle: Business executives do not understand true IT needs and are inspired by external vendors and other sources. The business dictates a solution, IT accepts it, and then

IT resources are consumed by the complexity of a non-optimal solution. There is pressure to deliver and consequently a high failure rate, rework rate, and, hence, low confidence in IT. This leads to further breakdown in IT business relationships and fuels more misaligned initiatives from an IT perspective.

This misaligned spiral just tends to get bigger with time and worsening economic cycles, similar to the unpredictable causes of tornadoes. Scientists are confused by nature—still unsure of the precise meteorological mechanisms that cause tornadoes to form. Although scientists understand the basic principles, the details remain a mystery. The rapid buildup of a tornado's dangerous combination of downdrafts, updrafts, and air convergence are not easily calculable. It's tough to break its occurrence when formed. Likewise, in order to break the spiral of IT adding low value or no value and for IT to be considered a true partner of the business, the IT organization needs to accurately estimate and fill demand. It needs a consolidated view of all types of demand (IT operations demand and IT development demand) to realize tradeoffs and synergies. This includes governance processes, metrics, and structures, as described in detail in chapter 4.

IT Strategy Alignment with Business Strategy

To understand the role that IT plays as an enabler and value partner, we need to start by looking at the following dynamics of the marketplace in the industry and the position of the company in that industry. How is the industry doing? What are the industry growth rates, industry margins and pricing, industry challenges like cost pressure or fear of substitute products and services, etc.? Leading companies are aggressively standardizing back office capabilities globally, so they can operate efficiently and free business unit leaders to focus on getting products to market faster. These companies typically build capabilities that disrupt or alter existing business models. And based on changing consumer dynamics and truly global competition, all businesses evaluate whether their capabilities are still creating a competitive advantage or should be moved to a shared-services model and managed for scale. Some companies tie this evaluation to the annual budgeting process or events like mergers or cost-cutting programs. This growing multiplicity of ways for IT to support strategies has exacerbated alignment and integration problems between IT and the business. It is very important for the IT leadership to understand and participate in this decision making of what to pursue as a company and how their capabilities will support that vision.

Governance/Funding/Organizational Capability

After this we should understand the IT operating model and how decisions are made, enforced, and tracked within the organization. This establishes an operational framework for running efficient and effective IT that is aligned with the business. This function is key for the planning and budgeting processes in the organization as well as making sure that IT spend is being managed as per the vision of the company.

> It is very important for the IT leadership to understand and participate in this decision making of what to pursue as a company and how their capabilities will support that vision.

A mature IT organization will typically establish the required structures, processes, metrics, and tools that facilitate IT decision making. The structures for such a function are dependent upon how federated or centralized the IT function is. For example, a company with many business units that are independent revenue generators will typically have IT spread out in those units to enable agility and nimbleness. A company that is more central and does not care so much for short time-to-market, on the other hand, could have IT centralized to make the enterprise decisions. The governance processes typically consist of strategic planning, project prioritization, project management, architecture and standards management, IT service delivery management, and IT financial monitoring. The metrics consist of key performance indicators that are indicative of the company-level levers. It could be some form of IT balanced scorecard that has financial, operations, projects, and customers measurement (e.g., service level management, etc.).

IT Processes

After we have looked at the above components, we also need to look at the processes used within their own organization—demand management, portfolio management, risks management, etc. The objective for IT leadership is to see how solution delivery and resource management processes are being managed to enhance the top line and the bottom line.

Aligning Business and IT— Business Architecture

People buy the shovel, but they want the hole.
—Unknown

Just like the captain of a ship uses a telescope to see where he needs to go, it is important to see the big picture before starting on the journey. Driving with a microscope may get you to your destination, but the journey will be slow and inefficient. Business IT alignment and integration arise from understanding across the enterprise what the company's business imperatives are. Business imperatives define the outcomes that the business must achieve to support its corporate strategies; they provide a clear view of a distant goal.

> Business IT alignment and integration arise from understanding across the enterprise what the company's business imperatives are.

Business imperatives are direct, actionable statements with measurable targets. Business imperatives provide direction for all key business decisions. They quantify the key priorities for the business in the near future and should be collected through business interviews with key stakeholders and leadership within the business.

Business imperatives provide the basis for developing IT technology imperatives and measuring the business impact of capabilities and solutions. Business imperatives should clearly communicate the strategic requirements that the organization must be prepared to support and should contain the following:

- Corporate mission statement and business strategies
- Business imperatives—These actionable statements should begin with "We must . . ." and define "what" must be

achieved, not "how." They should be measurable goals and should have a time line established for achieving these goals.
- Business priorities for achieving business imperatives
- Business challenges to achieving business imperatives

Once a coherent business direction is established and understood, the IT leadership needs to make sure they are enabling those strategies.

Each one of these aligned strategies will then result in the operational level goals and detailed tactics for the organization. So the typical questions to ask are: What is our strategic intent? How are we organized? What is our corporate culture? What do we view as our core competencies? What are our core business processes? What are the applications and infrastructures that support our processes and enable our strategy? How do we measure this performance?

Examples of Business Imperatives

1. Deliver *one company* to the marketplace. This could mean branding the company products as coming from one company if consumers are getting confused by the various products or service lines.

2. Build an *integrated view of the customers* across products or service lines. There has been a tremendous push by companies that sell a variety of products or services through different lines of businesses to combine all of the data and use that to gain a complete understanding of the customer—called the 360-degree view of the customer. This helps in cross-selling and up-selling activities. Chapter 3 on CRM details these capabilities.

3. Begin transformation toward being a total *information management solution* facilitator through a network of businesses. This can be evident in industries that sell products and their knowledge of products (i.e., intellectual property), which

can be combined across the value chain. For example, a cellular ground station can describe its current components and help configure its own upgrade or the components needed from the suppliers' value chain.

4. *Expand product/service portfolio* to expand sources of value. For example, an IT consulting firm needs to keep up with new services in areas like mobile computing, radio-frequency identification (RFID), cloud computing, etc. More and more companies these days are re-inventing products to incorporate services because information rich environments suggest the commoditization of everything. One common scheme for ducking the commodity bullet is to turn the products into a service and the existing services into a more context-rich service. When objects have intelligence and communication, every product becomes a potential platform through which companies can deliver service. For example, an auto can deliver navigational services while managing its own well being (OnStar). An earthmover can inform interested parties when the surface preparation is nearly complete so that the next stage of construction can begin. A printer can re-order ink before it runs out. Your medicine cabinet can remind you to take the right medicine on the right day.

5. Build capabilities to serve new customer segments as they become viable (e.g., a commercial bank expanding into retail banking).

6. Transform relationships from transactional to value-based relationships (e.g., a consulting firm charging a price-based on business outcomes).

The business architecture is then a view of the business that creates the business capabilities to achieve the business strategy. It has components of IT architecture—primarily of the application, information, and infrastructure architectures, as shown below.

Proper use of technology allows applications to manage information effectively, taking both data and context into account. IT capabilities thus support and enable business capabilities such as CRM, pricing, supply chain management (SCM), and back office optimization.

Figure 7: Business Capabilities Driving IT Capabilities

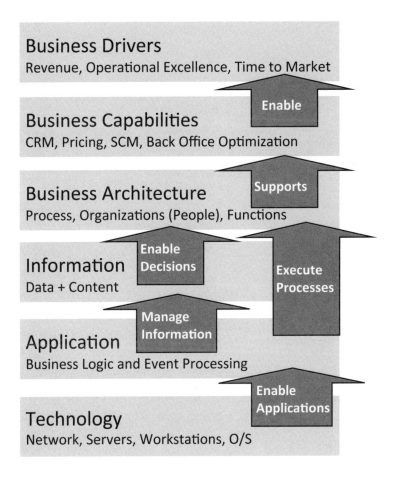

There is often a lack of comprehension, though, of how to "operationalize" these concepts and break the wall between strategy and execution. One of my good colleagues and a CIO himself once remarked, "When you walk into a restaurant and ask, 'Where's the bar?', they show you where the bar is and walk you there. They do not say, 'Here, read the process or the manual of how to get there.'" Creating this kind of customer-centric culture is key to clearly understanding internal and external customers and adding value accordingly. It is important to understand the flow from business to IT and how business architecture links long-range strategy to day-to-day execution.

Figure 8: Components of Business Capabilities

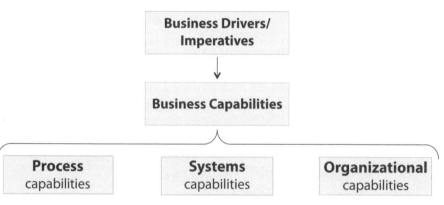

So a business capability integrates an organization's people, processes, and technology with its strategy. As shown in the figure above, this is a combination of business processes, organization structures, change management, and technology that represents an organization's ability to create value. Business drivers are determined by understanding the operating model of a company, the strategic forces in its market, the value chain model it supports, and the challenges it faces. Diagnosis of issues like cost-to-serve, time-to-market, margin pressure, etc. can help the company deter-

> So a business capability integrates an organization's people, processes, and technology with its strategy.

mine the right drivers needed. Once that is determined, the business capabilities can be determined in each piece of the value chain. Each one of those is then to be broken into process, systems, and organization capabilities. This book describes each one of these capabilities in different chapters. Process capabilities (as explained in chapter 3) need to look at the value chain in more depth. Each process then belongs to a certain domain within the value chain and has inputs, outputs, and a certain frequency of occurrence; the process provides opportunity for automation. System capabilities (as explained in chapter 3) are composed of applications, infrastructure, legacy and new technology platforms, etc. Organizational capabilities (as explained in chapter 3) are predominantly the composition of the human capital and the knowledge base in the company. It deals with issues of installation and adoption of processes and systems.

An example of business capabilities is explained below using the retail industry.

The retail industry is pretty broad in that the value chains work differently for different consumer products and goods. But there are certain trends that are common:

- "Retailization" is spreading as businesses across all industries vie for closer customer connections.
- Retail channels are continuing to blur and expand, generating new expectations from consumers and more cross-channel challenges for retailers.
- Shoppers are continuing to gravitate toward products and experiences that offer individual focus, interaction, customization, and cradle-to-grave offerings.
- Demand for online capabilities (and for a consistent experience) is increasing.
- Demographic shifts in spending power are driving retailers to rethink go-to-market strategies.

In these scenarios, when you begin analyzing the individual company needs, it is clear that winners will survive and gain market share by doing three things right:

- More focused customer strategy
- Aggressive adoption of analytics and closed loop measurement
- Relentless focus on agility and speed, from planning to execution

The winners in retail spend less money but target the customers more *scientifically* and execute their investments more *swiftly*.

The winners in retail spend less money but target the customers more *scientifically* and execute their investments more *swiftly*. To understand this, it is important to lay out the details of the value chain of the company. Finance, IT, human resources, and goods not for resale (GNFR) combine to manage the business, which consists of demand generation and demand fulfillment through various channels.

Figure 9: Example: Retail Capabilities

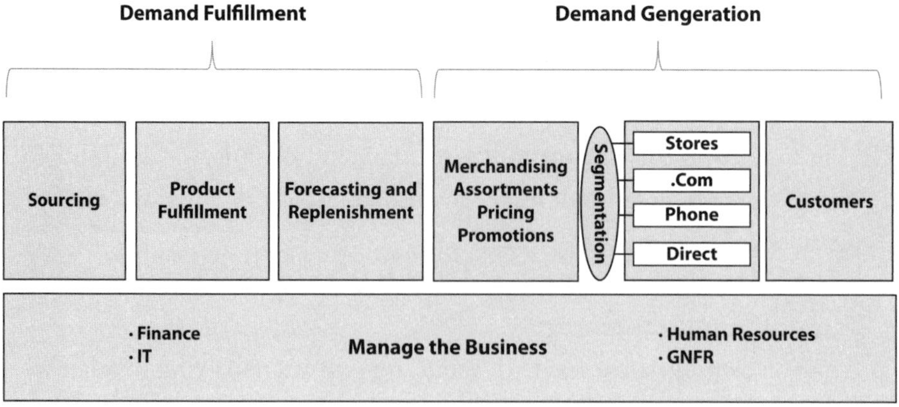

Demand Generation

Customers

Global trends indicate that purchasing activity is shifting away from aspirational channels and brands among middle and upper middle income brackets. Especially in economic slowdowns, there is a transition of spend toward discounters as well as lower cost brands and alternatives at all income levels. In economic slowdowns there is also increased interest in value through bundling. Retail market leaders need to be focused on leveraging data and information to target and profitably attract and retain their best customers, including data such as demographic, attitudinal, observational (visual tracking), and transactional (market basket and brand affinity). Companies need to have operating strategies and cultures that are willing to align offers and internal planning processes by segments.

They also need to be able to retract from unprofitable customers and be ready to abandon outdated vehicles or media when the data suggests that it's necessary. Almost everyone is familiar with the adage "Cut your losses," and many have also heard the full maxim, "Cut your losses and let your winners run." This is not a new idea; the phrase itself was first used by eighteenth-century British economist and trader David Ricardo. These were "golden rules" to Ricardo, and the actual wording was, "Cut short your losses" and "Let your profits run on." These are rules that we can continue to benefit from today, especially in the kind of business we pursue and the customers that constitute that market.

Channels

As shown in the following figure, there are many channels of products and services making it to the final consumer. Manufacturers may be providing these directly to the customer or they may have many intermediaries like agents, wholesalers, retailers, etc.

Figure 10: Channels of Distribution

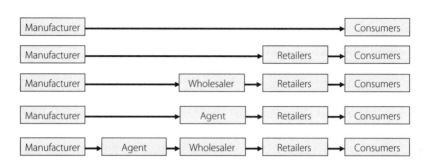

Channels and each intermediary shown above fulfill some important functions. They provide specialization and division of labor, provide economies of scale, and aid producers who lack resources to market directly. They also help in overcoming distribution constraints such as:

- *Temporal discrepancy*—A situation that occurs when a product is produced but a customer is not ready to buy it
- *Spatial discrepancy*—The difference between the location of a producer and the location of widely scattered markets
- *Discrepancy of quantity*—The difference between the amount of product produced and the amount an end user wants to buy
- *Discrepancy of assortment*—The lack of all the items a customer needs to receive full satisfaction from a product or products

Although channels are sometimes thought of as a cost, they can also be sources of competitive advantage. The key to remember is that a channel is not only a vehicle for physically moving goods but also involves the movement of titles, negotiation, promotion, and payment.

- The functions of a channel can't be eliminated. Somebody must do each function. Therefore, true disintermediation can never take place. Despite the fact that online companies like Amazon, eBay, etc. provide a direct link, they still have to manage those functions and do so more efficiently through the use of technology.

- Intensive distribution is rarely used with luxury products, and exclusive distribution is rarely used with convenience goods. Please note that levels of distribution intensity can range from *intensive distribution* to *selective distribution* to *exclusive distribution* depending upon product, market, and locations.
- Companies can either push or pull products through a channel.
- Competition, within a channel sense, can be horizontal, vertical, intertype, or system.
- Channels today are evolving, largely due to channel compression or consolidation.
- The number of SKUs provides a picture of the assortment provided by an organization. It is easy to visualize some stores with thirty to fifty thousand of them.

It is important for retailers to focus on some of the key functions performed in channels of distribution:

- *Buying*—Purchasing products from sellers for use or resale
- *Selling*—Ascertaining, activating, and satisfying the buyer's needs to the mutual continuous benefits of both buyer and seller
- *Sorting*—Performed by intermediaries to bridge discrepancies of assortment and quantity produced and demanded. Functions include sorting, accumulation, allocation, and assorting
- *Allocation*—Breaking down a homogenous supply into smaller and smaller lots
- *Grading*—Classifying by quality; often done via grade

labeling, though firms can grade their own products by private system (e.g., good, better, best)

- *Transportation*—Adding time and place utility to the product by moving it from where it was made to where it will be purchased and used. It includes all intermediate steps in the process.
- *Risk-taking*—Taking risks involved in transporting and owning products
- *Marketing research*—Collecting information (e.g., on market conditions, consumer trends, or competition)

Promotions/Marketing Mix Optimization

Marketing mix optimization is the application of statistical methodologies to measure the impact of marketing and media activities on revenue. Airlines and hotels have recently used concepts of yield management to optimize the marketing mix and markdown strategy for retailers. Statistical/econometric modeling is used to isolate key sales and marketing levers, while also accounting for noncontrollable factors that impact sales and/or the brand. These models can be used to:

- Quantify the effects of past marketing efforts.
- Provide an early warning to identify underperforming marketing efforts before they become too costly.
- Simulate many thousands of investment scenarios, thus allowing low-cost trials of marketing strategies.
- Optimize allocation of investment across any combination of marketing tactics. Also, within a specific marketing tactic, these models can help optimize allocation across products and geographies.
- Identify halo and cannibalization effects associated with media, promotion, and pricing tactics.
- Provide optimized marketing strategies that will ensure the best outcomes whatever the desired objectives.

In today's world, retailers have emerging media and technologies focused on analyzing customer-specific data and anticipating individual buyer behavior: Web 2.0 (interactive internet), mobile solutions, social networks (e.g., Facebook, Myspace), video game advertising, in-store visual tracking, and shelf monitoring.

Space and Assortment Optimization

As shown below, in a retail company, the value chain (logistics, supply chain, merchandizing, and customer touch points) can be handled more efficiently by the appropriate intelligence—applications and infrastructure to support areas like dynamic fulfillment, stock management, sourcing, space and assortment mix, advertising, pricing, and contact centers. Using application optimizers and data mining systems, performance accelerators that work on internal and external sources of information can lead to increased revenues, better margins, and better operations.

Figure 11: Scientific Retailing

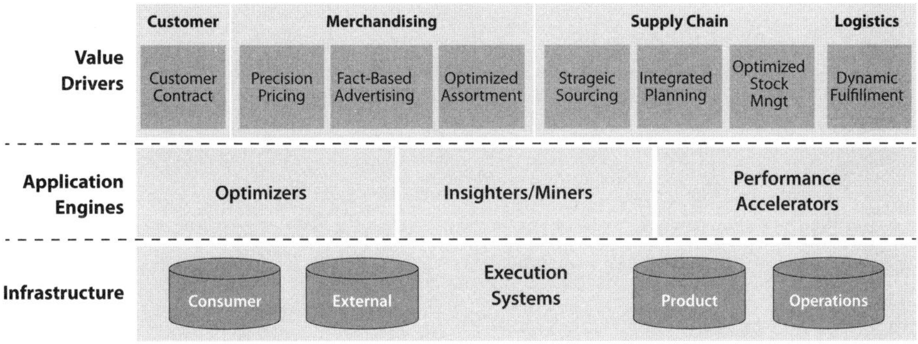

Value Drivers	Customer	Merchandising			Supply Chain			Logistics
	Customer Contract	Precision Pricing	Fact-Based Advertising	Optimized Assortment	Strageic Sourcing	Integrated Planning	Optimized Stock Mngt	Dynamic Fulfilment
Application Engines	Optimizers			Insighters/Miners		Performance Accelerators		
Infrastructure	Consumer	External		Execution Systems		Product		Operations

The basic components of these solutions from a systems perspective include the data, the models, "what if" scenario functionality, and optimization for planning. The data can be internal data, agency/media data, or third party data. The models are any applications that have statistical algorithms applied to input data that separates the portion of sales and profit due to each of the factors, sometimes using non-linear programming. Simulation and optimizations are not models but are mathematical solutions that best allocate budgets to drive different results including sales and/or brand. Optimizations can be run at varying levels (national vs. regional) and with relevant constraints.

To recap, in this example we saw how understanding the business processes and value chain is important for understanding how to build business capabilities. Further, we saw how IT helps execute the building of those business capabilities.

Focus #1: Process Capabilities

People forget how fast you did a job,
but they remember how well you did it.

—Howard W. Newton, American advertising executive and author

Over the long term, only one out of every five process transformation efforts reaches its financial and strategic objectives. This is a statistic that was yielded by countless surveys from the world's leading consulting firms:

- "Eighty percent of companies that sought to solve their strategic issues by process engineering had neither 'met nor exceeded' their expectations."—Mercer Consulting
- Of one hundred British firms that had embarked on "improvement programs for their operating and organizational models, only 20 percent yielded tangible financial results."—A.T. Kearney
- Improperly executed process re-engineering efforts are characterized by "unexpected long-term side effects such as declining morale, loss of motivation, erosion of trust and weakened teamwork."—D. Rigby, *Planning Review*, 1993
- "Eighty-seven percent of re-engineering projects had failed to solve the true strategic issues."—Holland and Kumar, 1995

In a rapidly changing world, the traditional sources of competitive advantage no longer provide a lasting edge. New products and new technologies are duplicated quickly. Processes, on the other hand, are a source of sustainable competitive advantage. They are difficult to duplicate, and, when well designed and well managed, they provide a means for coping with change. A good product, for example, has a limited life span in the marketplace. A good

> A good product, for example, has a limited life span in the marketplace. A good product development *process*, however, enables a company to create appealing new products over and over again.

product development *process*, however, enables a company to create appealing new products over and over again. Furthermore, well-designed processes can accommodate and compensate for variations in human resources. By linking several processes according to the product or service flow within the organization, the company can establish an end-to-end holistic view of its parts. This allows for breaking through existing organizational silos.

In addition, processes help to focus on the internal and external customers. As one of the CIOs I recently met mentioned,

> Our business conditions are typically fluid and so our process needs to be dynamic, iterative, and participatory. The process knowledge also helps with concepts of planning and analyses, and these are synergistic and not separate and distinct activities. With the process, we can play "What if?" games and look to model business scenarios to reflect the dynamic nature of our business to explore more than one set of possibilities.

A process is a succession of logically related actions that deliver a certain outcome with added value for the customer (internal or external). They are triggered by business events, such as a customer order. How you take that order, capture it, and deliver the products/ services decides your company's position vis-à-vis the competition. Processes have two important characteristics:

- They have defined start and end points (with inputs and outputs as needed).
- They have a series of distinct actions focused on creating the desired outcome.

Processes can be broken down into hierarchies as depicted below. This kind of visual depiction makes it easy to brainstorm the value of each activity and helps with improving quality at the macro level. As shown below, each process step can be broken down into sub-processes and more steps within. The key is to get to a level where tasks and activities can be seen visually.

Figure 12: Process Hierarchy

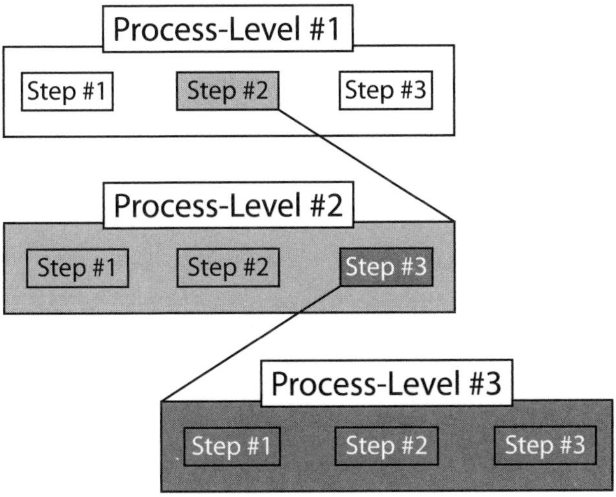

The actual flow within the process can be a physical flow (the product itself) or a logical flow (information flows). The design of a process illustrates both flows in one graphical representation. It builds a capability representation. A capability is a logical grouping of functional and support processes, where functional processes are one link in the value chain. The value chain delivers value for the external customer. The begin and end point of the functional process, however, can be related to internal or external customers. Support processes, meanwhile,

> The actual flow within the process can be a physical flow (the product itself) or a logical flow (information flows).

are typically processes that do not create direct added value for the external customers. They are, however, required to enable functional processes. They often cross organizational boundaries. The customers of support processes are in most cases internal customers. An example of a support process is the selection process within the HR department.

Different levels are defined to represent the hierarchy within the type of action.

- **Level 0: Framework** (platforms and capabilities) and end-to-end process level.
- **Level 1: Process level** (functional and support processes), a group of similar actions performed by different groups of people (teams) within one capability.
- **Level 2: Sub-process level**, variations applied to a process.
- **Level 3: Activity level**, where activities are initiated by one or more events and answer the questions who, when, how, and with what? It describes the actions of one or more persons who are part of a team.
- **Level 4: Task level**, where tasks are atomic activities and are used to describe the actions of one person (or object) in one place at one time. **Note:** practitioners of service oriented architecture (SOA) who try to design systems often struggle with the granularity of services to define—trading off between performance or scalability and abstraction for reuse. This exercise in process engineering, in which you get to the level of individual tasks, is key to understanding how coarse or fine grained the services need to be. This is elaborated more in chapter 3, System Capabilities.
- **Level 5: Work instruction level**, where work instructions give detailed guidelines on how to perform the action explained in the task level.

In this hierarchy, the actual action performance, which is done by one or more persons, is described at Level 3, the activity level. The general task description is performed at the lowest level, Level 4. Tasks consist of work instructions; work instructions are a detailed description of what is required to perform the task. While designing a process, it is not sufficient just to put actions in a logical order. It is fundamental to understand why the process is there in the first place and how all the involved parties can benefit the most from this process.

> It is fundamental to understand why the process is there in the first place and how all the involved parties can benefit the most from this process.

Different approaches exist to achieve excellent processes. Business process improvement (BPI) is an approach to achieving excellent processes that focuses primarily on making incremental improvements to existing processes, aiming at long-lasting advances. Often the key for improvement is found in small process adaptations, referred to as "quick wins."

In fact, financial guru, radio host, and bestselling author Dave Ramsey recommends a similar approach for his debt reduction plan. Rather than tackling the largest debts first, he urges his listeners and readers to start with the smallest debts in order to make immediate changes, gain confidence, and build momentum. "You need some quick wins in order to stay pumped enough to get out of debt completely," Ramsey writes in an article on his website, www.DaveRamsey.com. He states, "Paying the little debts off first gives you quick feedback, and you are more likely to stay with the plan." Quick wins, though small, can help create lasting change.

Quick wins through BPI are effective in achieving localized improvements in narrowly defined areas and tend to involve relatively low-cost, low-risk projects. Although a quick win looks like a small and easy intervention, the impact on the process can be a real relief for the process. Continuous improvement is realized by continuously looking for new process improvement opportunities. Each implementation of an improvement opportunity adds durable value to the existing process. Process improvement techniques can deliver tremendous value; however, there are limits to doing the same thing better. This principle is used for improving existing processes as part of continuous improvement.

Business process reengineering (BPR) is the fundamental reexamination, redesign, and implementation of a process or a set of processes. It typically means starting from a clean slate and looking for ways to maximize the value creation potential of the enterprise end-to-end processes. Although BPR is a good technique, it should be mentioned that consequently implementing changes through BPR requires higher investments than through Process Improvement techniques. The reason for this is that BPR has a much higher impact on the organization, applications, and other processes. As has been highlighted in numerous industry studies and books like *Reengineering the Corp* (Hammer and Champy), BPR is typically used for creating new processes or for updating existing processes since it rethinks the entire value chain to improve how business is conducted. It involves major changes to a business's key processes as opposed to merely incremental improvements. Successful re-engineering requires a shift from function to process. In the first stage of transition, functions drive the business. In the second stage, processes are acknowledged, but functions still dominate. In the third stage, processes drive the business.

BPR is defined as "the *fundamental* rethinking and *radical* redesign of business processes to achieve *dramatic improvements* in critical, contemporary measures of performance, such as cost, quality, service, and speed." Therefore, it looks at the essentials of the process, such as why the work is done, who does it, where it is done, and when. After these questions are answered, the next step is to examine the process's ability to add value.

Whether you look at process improvements or process re-engineering, an excellent process has an output that creates value for the customer and therefore provides a means of competitive advantage. An inefficient process creates the opposite effect—diminished value and competitive disadvantage. The characteristics to achieve process excellence are summarized as follows:

Adds value for the customer
Processes produce outcomes that create value for customers and, ultimately, for the organization and its stakeholders. When a customer can choose between similar products or services, he or she will choose the one that gives the highest level of satisfaction (why do people prefer Starbucks over very similar coffee in so many other places?). Process design should begin with the customer's viewpoint. An understanding of what the customer truly values should drive the definition of outcomes that the business must produce. Those outcomes should in turn be used to define the organization's processes. As a result, excellent processes will make the company "easy to do business with."

Eliminates waste
Value generates profit, and waste stands for cost. A customer is willing to pay for things that have added value for him. When buying a stamp, a customer is willing to pay for the stamp so her letter will arrive at the designated address. Getting the letter to the designated addressee adds value to the customer. All the work that does not add value for the customer when it comes to buying a stamp and mail delivery should be reduced to an absolute minimum. A process perspective *focuses on value, business results, and outcomes*, rather than on activities and tasks. A process perspective views the customer as the fundamental definer of value and as the reason that processes exist in the first place.

Has a documented design
Processes have to be maintainable. Poorly documented processes will limit the level of transparency and will increase the danger of the process evolving without control. Process documentation, however, is not an objective in itself.

Is simple and yet flexible
Competitive markets are subject to change. A company can only keep its sustainable advantage by staying on track with market changes. Therefore, simple and flexible processes are critical success factors to maintain or improve the market position. They allow the company to quickly adapt to the current situation.

Compresses time
Time is often considered as a big cost. Therefore, time saving is a direct form of cutting costs. Customers like their products to be delivered on time, they like to get their orders fast, they like fast after-sales service, and they dislike waiting in line.

Has clear links to other processes
The way processes interact with each other should be clear. In this way, one creates an overview of the impact a process has on its related processes. Clear links will allow an end-to-end view across business and service units. They integrate processes with the bigger picture.

Is user friendly (repeatable and unambiguous)
Processes are designed to deliver a certain outcome, but they are also operated. Operating a process in an optimized way can only be done when the user is able to follow the process instructions.

Has a process owner
Process owners have an end-to-end responsibility for achieving the

predefined process outcomes. They take care of all the required actions to keep processes excellent.

Is measurable
Measurable processes can be evaluated; this evaluation is the input for process improvements.

Is geared to some golden rules or a vision
Golden rules should be defined before designing and analyzing the process. They are used to keep the process focus right. Take the example of a customer service center where the process to handle customers' calls needs to be redesigned. A golden rule can be: "Maximize client satisfaction" or "Optimize amount of calls treated per hour." Depending on the chosen goal, the process focus will be different. For "maximizing client satisfaction," the focus will be on training the workforce on products and customer queries. But to "optimize calls per hour," the training will be geared toward information retrieval and closing calls only.

Process Development Roles and Responsibilities

Since process management is a discipline that provides a holistic end-to-end view of the compete business and a clear operating model with all involved parties, there should be defined roles for a team putting together such a view for the enterprise.

- **Process Owner/Sponsor**

    The process owner and sponsor have responsibility for a cluster of related processes, so he or she needs to act in the interest of the organization and not in the favor of one specific business or service unit. When cross-departmental disputes are escalated up to the framework level, it is the process owner who will close the issues. So the process sponsor needs to function as the link to relate the processes to the business strategy.

Process sponsors are also responsible for understanding and communicating the purpose and overall procedures to adhere to process steps. They should be conversant with the dependencies of a set of processes to other processes and will be the point of contact for future updates to the process.

- **Process Design Teams**

  The process design team is responsible for the design of the process. This team has members who understand the business domain very well and can translate business needs into functional requirements. Typical business analysts with an understanding of business process modeling can work well in this role. Companies typically use tools and techniques such as BPMN (as detailed in the following section), Microsoft Visio, or other modeling tools from software companies. They provide the adequate representation to appropriately design processes and all supporting documents.

- **Process Excellence Board**

  There should be a group responsible for maintaining consistent process detail through process design standards, maintaining standard templates for process deliverables, and approving all processes as presented by process design teams.

Business Process Modeling

Just like there is a need for a language to be able to communicate, share ideas, and disperse knowledge, process design needs some standard notation so it is commonly understood. Business process modeling notation (BPMN) is used in many organizations as a common language for designing and managing processes. It is a standard to describe business process flows. It is now called business process model and notation and was developed by the business process management initiative (BPMI). It is currently being maintained by the object management group (OMG) since the two organizations merged in 2005. The first goal of BPMN is to provide a notation that is easily understandable by all business users.

BPMN defines a business process diagram (BPD), which is based on a flowcharting technique tailored for creating graphical models of business process operations. A process design is a network of graphical objects called actions (i.e., work). These actions are represented in a logical order called flows. A BPD is made up of a set of graphical elements. These elements enable the easy development of simple diagrams that will look familiar to most business analysts (e.g., a flowchart diagram). The elements were chosen to be distinguishable from each other and to utilize shapes that are familiar to most modelers. For example, actions are rectangles and decisions are diamonds. It should be emphasized that one of the drivers for the development of BPMN is to create a simple mechanism for creating business process designs, while at the same time being able to handle the complexity inherent to business processes. The approach taken to handle these two conflicting requirements was to organize the graphical aspects of the notation into specific categories. This provides a small set of notation categories so that the reader of a BPD can easily recognize the basic types of elements and understand the diagram. Within the basic notation categories, additional variation and information can be added to support the requirements for complexity without dramatically changing the basic look and feel of the diagram. There are seven basic notation categories (they are explained in more detail in the next section):

- Event
- Action (process, sub-process, activity, and task)
- Decision point
- Connector
- Swim lane
- Artifact
- Horizontal discipline

BPMN Elements
Event

An event is something that "happens" during the course of a business process. These events affect the flow of the process and usually have a cause (trigger) or an impact (result). Events are circles with open centers to allow internal markers to differentiate different triggers or results. There are three types of events, based on when they affect the flow: start, intermediate, and end.

Element	Description
Start Event	As the name implies, the start event indicates where a particular process will start. In terms of sequence flow, a start event starts the process flow; hence a start event will have no incoming flows (sequence flows cannot arrive at start events).
Intermediate Event	Intermediate events occur between a start event and an end event. They will affect the flow of the process, but they will not start or (directly) terminate the process.

Element	Description
End Event	As the name implies, the end event indicates where a particular process will end. In terms of sequence flow, an end event finishes the process flow; hence an end event will have no outgoing flows (sequence flows cannot start from end events).

Actions (i.e., Process, Sub-Process, Activity, and Task)

An action is a generic term for work that the company performs. It can be atomic or nonatomic (compound). The word "action" is used to refer to the symbol used for process, sub-process, activity, and task, without referring to the specified level.

Element	Description
Process	Referring to the functional process framework, a process is a group of similar actions performed by different groups of people (teams) within one capability (e.g., distribute mail). Process flows are used to represent the flow between processes; on this level only actions are used—no decision points yet.
Sub-Process	A process is split into sub-processes because a variation is applied to a process (e.g., distribute unaddressed newspapers).
Activity	An activity is initiated by one or more events and answers to the questions who, when, how, and with what? It describes the actions of one or more persons who are part of a team (e.g., drop mail for delivery point).
Task	A task is an atomic activity and is used to describe the actions of one person (or object) in one place at one time (e.g., put mail in mailbox).
Exploded Action	This means that the action has a more detailed description on a lower level. A "plus" sign in the lower center of the shape indicates that the action is an exploded action and has a lower level of detail.

Decision Point

Decision point is a place in the process where the flow takes a set of options based on criteria that are used as inputs.

Element	Description
Decision Point	Decision points are used to control the divergence of sequence. Decision points direct the flow toward a specific direction in the process.

Connector

Events, actions, and decision points are connected together in a diagram to create the basic skeletal structure of a business process. There are three *connecting objects* that provide this function.

Element	Description
Sequence Flow	A sequence flow is used to show the sequence of the actions in a process.
Message Flow	A message flow is used to show the flow of messages between two participants that are prepared to send and receive them. In BPMN, two separate pools in the diagram will represent the two participants (e.g., business entities or business roles). Pools are explained in more detail in the next paragraph.
Association	An association is used to associate information with flow objects. Text and graphical objects can be associated with them.

Swim Lane

Swim lanes are used as a mechanism to organize actions into separate visual categories in order to illustrate different functional capabilities or responsibilities.

Element	Description
Pool	A pool represents a participant in the process. A participant can be a specific business entity (e.g., a company) or can be a more general business role (e.g., a buyer, seller, or manufacturer). Graphically, a pool is a container for partitioning a process from other pools when modeling business-to-business situations. A pool, however, does not need any internal details (i.e., it can be a "black box").
Lane	Lanes are used to organize and categorize actions within a pool. The meaning of the lanes is up to the modeler. BPMN does not specify the usage of lanes. Lanes are often used for such things as internal roles (e.g., manager, associate), systems (e.g., an enterprise application), an internal department (e.g., shipping, finance), etc. In addition, lanes can be nested or defined in a matrix. For example, there could be an outer set of lanes for company departments and then an inner set of lanes for roles within each department.

Swim lanes can be compared with the lanes of a swimming pool. They look like the straight long tracks in the pool. Only one swimmer is allowed per lane, where she can perform multiple actions. The swimmer cannot leave her lane, but she can communicate with other swimmers.

Artifact

Artifacts provide additional context appropriate to a specific modeling situation. Any number of artifacts can be added to a diagram as appropriate for the context of the processes being modeled.

Element	Description
Data Object	In BPMN, a data object is considered an artifact as it does not have any direct affect on the sequence of the process, but it does provide information about what the process does—that is, how documents, data, and other elements are used and updated during the process. In some cases, the data object will be shown being sent from one action to another, via a sequence flow. Data objects will also be associated with message flow. They are not to be confused with the message itself, but could be thought of as the "payload" or content of some messages. In other cases, a data object will be shown as being an input or an output of a process.
Information	Text annotations are a mechanism for a modeler to provide additional information for the reader of a BPMN diagram. The information artifact can be connected to a specific object on the diagram with an association, but it does not affect the flow of the process. Text associated with the information artifact can be placed within the bounds of the open rectangle.
Data Store	The data store artifact can be used to indicate whenever a link is made with a database (CMDB—configuration management database, etc.)
Application	The application artifact can be used to indicate when a link is made with an application. An application represents a certain module, screen, function, a program, a group of programs, etc.

Horizontal Discipline

A horizontal discipline can be used to group an amount of actions that belong to the same functional discipline. It has only a documentation purpose and has no influence on the process flow.

An Example—Procure-to-Pay Process

As discussed in the business architecture section, it is important for the organization to know what capabilities to build in order to seek a competitive advantage. And there is a lot of talk in the industry that companies have engineered process capabilities so rigidly that changing them at times creates disruptions. Joanne Sammer and Mike Costa in *Business Finance* wrote,

> Unlike many systems, ERP suites are designed under the assumption that an organization will modify its business processes to suit the software, rather than the other way around. ERP systems work most effectively in an organization that integrates processes across all parts of the enterprise, freely shares information, and uses common terminology. You have to step back from ERP and realize that its success lies as much with business process re-engineering and standardizing business rules and processes as it does with the software.

The way to look at *process capabilities* is that they need to be viewed end-to-end. Then, at each sub-process level, you need to see what will add value and how, after removing redundancies, you can create a flow that will provide flexibility and value. The first thing to understand is that leading organizations take a holistic view of their *procure-to-pay* process. Efficiencies can be created by understanding how each sub-process step has an impact on the overall process.

- The entire procurement process (from purchase requisition to payment) is captured in a single system to deliver end-to-end processing capability. This improves audit and reporting capabilities and also improves the ability to estimate commitments. The administration of users and approvals in one system enables data quality to be achieved much more easily than through disparate systems—this results in a reduction in rework, errors, and processing costs.

- All data kept in the central repository is available to the entire organization. This improves supplier compliance (monitoring/reporting), and supplier performance can be measured and managed more efficiently.
- Supplier assessment is based on a total cost of ownership (TCO) analysis with insight into long-range costs. This enables much more efficient administration of negotiated contracts (for example, quicker release of a purchase order [PO], as pricing is already known).
- Easy access to and strict enforcement of procurement policies—this improves understanding of policies and increases compliance.

The key is to understand that when thinking of process and process design there needs to be an understanding of the value levers, and those become the "golden rules" of thinking how to lay the process out. For the *procure-to-pay* process, these typically are:

- **Operating expense efficiency**—This is achieved by sourcing effectiveness and following regulatory compliance. Also, operating costs can be reduced by process efficiency as a lever as shown in the following figure.
- **Working capital efficiency**—This refers to optimization of payment terms (e.g., getting payment within thirty days instead of sixty days).

So the *procure-to-pay* process of any company's supply chain at a high level has several steps. First the purchase order is processed and submitted to vendors. The company then receives the order and manages the goods and services. Finally, an invoice is sent and payment is processed. Suppliers must be managed throughout this process.

Figure 13: Procure-to-Pay Process

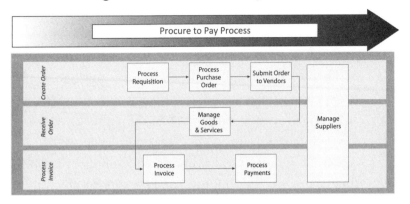

- **Process Requisition**—This is a standardized and flexible requisition process across the organization.
- **Process Purchase Order**—This is a standard approval process and workflow to create Orders from Requisitions.
- **Submit Orders**—This is a process to streamline communication to and from suppliers.
- **Manage Goods and Services**—This is a flexible receipt process that handles materials and services in a timely manner.
- **Process Invoice**—This is a process in which the accounts payable (AP) service center leverages purchasing and receipt documents to process invoices.
- **Process Payment**—This is a timely and accurate payment process.
- **Manage Suppliers**—This is a process that institutionalizes a proactive supplier management program.

As depicted above, this is the Level 1 view of the process and needs to be detailed into sub-processes for an understanding of the flow of work and the flow of information. The following is an explanation of the ways that an organization can improve the end-to-end process at every sub-process level.

Process Requisition **Sub-Process:**

In many organizations, utilization of electronic requisitions and workflow capabilities speeds up the initial phase of the procurement cycle.

- Make available an electronic, standard requisition process to appropriate members of the organization. This improves reporting of spend, commitments, and accruals.
- Code financial information (general ledge [GL], cost center, project, etc.) at the time of request rather than at the time of invoice. This improves and streamlines downstream processing of financial transactions and ensures appropriate commitment accounting and reporting.
- Integrate standard workflow routing with auto-generated notification into systems. This improves the reporting processes to review requisitions and their approvals. It also shortens the time to receive approvals and helps create an electronic approval audit trail for reporting and analysis.
- Approve purchase transactions all at once and at the time of requisition. This reduces cycle time from request to order to payment. It also eliminates unnecessary approvals and redundant activities.
- Rationalize approval limits based on financial control requirements. This will reduce approval rules maintenance.

Process Purchase Order **Sub-Process:**

The company should utilize contract purchasing, blanket POs, and other direct purchasing methods where applicable to minimize the volume of purchase orders and speed up the cycle time to create, approve, and process POs. Mature organizations measure success by their overall tracking of the reduction in procurement transaction costs.

- Use of procurement cards where appropriate (e.g., low dollar and high volume) helps reduce the number of POs, which reduces purchasing cycle time. This also allows purchasing and finance teams to focus their analyses efforts on high transaction amount areas where value can be added.

- Contract purchasing and blanket POs help reduce approval and transaction execution time as well as the redundant work effort involved. The ability to review supplier spend across the organization will provide insights into current spend and yield opportunities to leverage purchasing power.

- The IT systems help maintain the current and timely status of orders (and change orders). This facilitates downstream transaction processing, improves data quality, and improves reporting capabilities (up-to-date commitments).

Submit Order to Vendor Sub-Process:

- Automate document delivery to suppliers via auto-fax, email, EDI, XML, etc. Direct data entry into systems will reduce time and effort to process transactions and communicate with vendors. Reduction in paper processing will save administrative work associated with printing and mailing purchase orders. This also standardizes the process to deliver documents to vendors and reduces manual processing time.

- Commit to e-procurement/commerce to facilitate cross-enterprise communication. This facilitates real-time data availability and minimizes the need to place cross-company phone calls to check and track the status of orders, reducing buyer involvement in transactions.

Manage Goods and Services Sub-Process:

- Utilize material and service receipt functionality to facilitate reporting and downstream processing. Timely entry improves inventory accounting and facilitates downstream invoice transaction and processing.

- Utilize evaluated receipt settlement (ERS) capabilities where appropriate and with specific suppliers since this eliminates the need for invoicing and invoice entry. This was pioneered by General Motors (GM) to save the company time and money. Major benefits of ERS include invoice variance prevention, the elimination of non-value-added work (like tasks associated with reconciliation), and opportunity cost of capital savings.
- Standardize inventory receipt and the accounting process across the organization. This provides all interested parties (such as business units or accounts payable [AP]) visibility into the payment process.

Process Invoice **Sub-Process:**

- Centralize accounts payable responsibilities across the entire organization and process all AP transactions through a single system. This reduces overall cost and enables timely recognition of liability. It also minimizes administration of approvals (which should be at point of purchase—the process requisition stage).
- Reduce paper invoices and checks—request electronic invoices from vendors and pay vendors via electronic fund transfer (EFT). It reduces processing and administrative costs and lowers the risk of processing errors.
- Scan and route 100 percent of invoices when received by the AP processing center. Apart from reducing the quantity of paper records, it facilitates routing to the payables system.
- Use drill-down capabilities within systems to gather information regarding procurement (including drill-down to scanned image). This speeds up analysis and reconciliation time line.

Process Payments **Sub-Process:**

- Consolidate multiple invoices or payments to one vendor into a single EFT or check to reduce the number of invoices requiring data entry, reduce handling of paper checks, reduce check reconciliation efforts, and improve data quality and reporting.

- Utilize EFT/automatic clearing house (ACH) for payment to reduce use of paper checks, since this limits system and human resource requirements for check reconciliation and offers a better insight into cash flow through understanding of an expected float.

- Eliminate manual check request generation to improve financial reporting capabilities and financial audit trails. It also reduces processing time and approval time.

- Raise the limit for checks requiring multiple signatures (specifically if consolidating vendor payments) but provide high disbursement reports to AP managers weekly. This increases the payment cycle time and reduces the time executives spend reviewing and signing checks.

Manage Suppliers **Sub-Process:**

- Suppliers are reviewed and approved at the time when the vendor is selected. Preferred supplier programs should be put in place to leverage buying power. Consolidated spend will drive purchasing power across the enterprise, which will reduce costs. The strategic sourcing group will have a better view of cross-organizational spending patterns.

- Centralize vendor records for better maintenance and enforcement of new supplier procedures. This will enable easier analysis of supplier relationships, speed transaction processing, and ensure appropriate handling of product returns and credit memos. Also, the procurement organization should equip suppliers with self-service tools to reduce administrative tasks such as payment status inquiries, etc.

- Establish clearly defined master data processes, procedures, and policies across the organization. This limits the number of active vendor master records in the system and ensures appropriate compliance with vendor contracts. It also facilitates real-time supplier reporting.

- Establish an organization-wide supplier performance measurement system enabling suppliers to track key metrics and take corrective action as necessary. This improves supplier performance and compliance. It also encourages open dialogue with the supplier to help solidify key supplier relationships.

- Measure suppliers against internal and external benchmarks and establish a continuous improvement program with suppliers that will reward or penalize suppliers based on performance. This provides management with data to choose which suppliers to enter into strategic relationships with and which relationships to terminate.

Process Excellence with Lean and Six Sigma

Tell me and I will forget, show me and
I may remember, involve me and I'll understand.
—Chinese Proverb

If you can't describe what you are doing
as a process, you don't know what you're doing
—W. Edwards Deming, father of the quality revolution,
author of *Out of the Crisis, 14 Points for Management*

Across many industries there is some confusion between how Lean and Six Sigma are different or similar. The way to look at it is that Lean is the management philosophy and Six Sigma is a great set of tools that help you chart your path. You can use *Six Sigma* to reduce variation, but you would use *Lean management* to take your processes to a new level altogether.

Six Sigma translates a real-world problem into a statistical problem, finds a statistical solution, and translates this back into the real world. In statistics, the variability, or deviation, of a process is symbolized by the Greek letter Sigma (σ). Six Sigma focuses on reducing this process variation to the point that no defects are produced.

> Six Sigma translates a real-world problem into a statistical problem, finds a statistical solution, and translates this back into the real world.

	Lean	Six Sigma
Driver	Remove waste	Reduce variation
Assumption	Waste removal will improve business performance	Removing structural root causes will ensure lasting improvements

75

	Lean	Six Sigma
Focus	Value creation in every activity	Ensure process output meets customer requirements continuously
Approach	Eliminate actions that add no value for the customer	Quantify the impact of parameters on the process output

Six Sigma is about supporting different situations with different and specific tools. Lean is about looking for efficient solutions and reducing waste.

So What is Lean?

Yes, Lean is just that: "lean." More efficient muscle and less redundant fat. It is a business philosophy that shortens the time line between the customer order and the shipment of that product to the customer by eliminating waste (non-value-adding activities).

In the late 1800s, cars were built on blocks in the barn as workers walked around the cars. These were built by craftsmen with pride and the passion of creating a product that excels. The components were hand-crafted and hand-fitted, with excellent quality. Needless to say, only a few cars were produced, and they were very expensive. This was called *craft manufacturing*. This was a technique used since man first appeared on this planet, when our remote ancestors made weapons and tools by chipping rocks. The process required one person to have the skill and the right materials. Each stone tool was hand-crafted when it was needed.

Then in the 1920s, after the time and motion studies by Fredrick Taylor, the concept of the *assembly line* was birthed. Henry Ford was able to hire low-skilled laborers for simplistic jobs. Then Eli Whitney designed a manufacturing system that used interchangeable parts. If one craftsman were to make a musket, he could adjust the fittings to suit variations in the stock or barrel. Typical manufacturing required skilled engineers to finish assembling products by making the pieces fit together. In Whitney's 1799 contract with the US Army, the low price was possible because he planned to minimize these variations and eliminate the final adjustments. Eli Whitney's interchangeable parts idea was used for cars, and the number of vehicles produced was huge. Cars were finally affordably priced for the average family. This was called *mass manufacturing*. With the rise of global markets and competition from foreign companies, manufacturers across the world began to look at their production processes more closely.

At the same time, the advent of the quality movement in Japan and the concept of flexible assembly lines began. A great weakness in any Ford factory was the time required to change from making one product to another. Ford, therefore, needed to maximize batch sizes in order to minimize downtime. Toyota drastically reduced setup times so that multiple small batches made nearly as efficient use of the machinery as larger batches. At Toyota, all these innovations led to greater change in the factory workforce. Along with increased automation, this paved the way for cell-based manufacturing. These flexible assembly line units were called cells, and these involved highly skilled workers with broader jobs offering more variety in work. This was a paradigm shift, and despite being counterintuitive it led to decreased costs through process improvements. This was called *lean manufacturing*. In fact, the term "lean" was coined to describe the "Toyota Production System" by John Krafcik, one of the research members on Jim Womack's MIT (Massachusetts Institute of Technology) team for the five-year study that led to the seminal book, *The Machine that Changed the World*.

Many companies still find themselves stuck partway between mass and lean production. The problem is that most managers view additions to scientific knowledge in small, incremental improvements. They just aren't trained to make the quantum leaps

> Many companies still find themselves stuck partway between mass and lean production.

in thinking that are needed. The Toyota Production Method is about learning—the culture of science—continuous learning. Mass production models focus on exploiting economies of scale and use organizational hierarchies with a pyramid of untrained workers at the bottom. A lean manufacturing enterprise thinks more about its customers than it does about running big machines fast to absorb labor and overhead. The lean enterprise has a flat, team-based structure, with a high degree of work autonomy. By the nature of the work, a lean enterprise develops highly trained, motivated employees.

One VP of operations recently summed it up:

When I first went to a Lean training, I thought I had stumbled into a religious revival meeting. "You must lead them across Jordan to the promised land," said one keynote speaker. "Take heart, you can do this." And even when we had begun to apply Lean in our business, the next thing you discover is that it's not enough. You've got to build a lean enterprise: from accounting, to upper management, to the shipping docks. If you can manage that, and many companies have, then you still have to target your suppliers, and politely convince them—or outright order them—to get lean.

This management philosophy believes in the elimination of waste in processes, and the whole philosophy centers around five principles: value, value stream, flow, pull, and perfection.

- *Value*—What the customer wants to buy. Value is simply defined as profitably meeting or exceeding the customer's requirements and expectations. Whether a company manufactures physical products, develops software, or provides services, the thought process of who creates value needs to be understood from the customer's perspective. When you think of what customers want, it impacts the way you create those products or services. Typically the customer wants you to solve his or her problem completely and reduce the number of decisions he or she must make to solve the problem. Customers want to get to the final state without wasting their time and want to be provided exactly what

> Whether a company manufactures physical products, develops software, or provides services, the thought process of who creates value needs to be understood from the customer's perspective.

they want in the most optimal experience. In fact, more and more these days, with a mature customer who has too many options for anything that he or she needs, the process evolves as follows:

> » I want to *know*: Information
> » I want to *have*: Transaction
> » I want to *interact*: Relationship
> » I want to be *engaged*: Immersion

- **Value stream**—This describes the process of how that "value" is delivered in the current state of the company. So the value stream is an end-to-end process that delivers a product or service to a customer. The process steps along the way may both use and produce intermediate goods, services, and information to reach that primary end. By locating the value creating processes next to one another and by processing one unit at a time, work flows smoothly from one step to another and finally to the customer. This includes all the value-added activities as well as some redundant and non-value-added activities that go into producing the end product or service. The value-added activity is any activity that increases the market form or function of the product or service. These are things the customer is willing to pay for. For example, in the airline industry, actual flying time is something that the customer is really paying for. Or in the healthcare industry, the customer is really paying for the diagnosis and/or treatment. And the non-value-added activities are those that do not add market form or function or are not necessary. These activities should be eliminated, simplified, reduced, or integrated. For example, in the airline industry, no customer wants to be waiting in line for checking in or boarding the plane.

- *Flow*—Organizing value-added steps in proper sequence. The "flow" or "value stream" perspective represents a shift from vertical to horizontal thinking, which exists in companies as corporate functions. Flow is enabled when materials and processes are standardized across the supply chain to reduce complexity.
- *Pull*—Triggering flow from the customer's needs (e.g., have only projects in IT that the pipeline can take—that is, demand management).
- *Perfection*—Continuous improvement.

So the basic foundation of Lean is the focus on eliminating and reducing waste. The fundamental concept is rather simple: execute work in a way that waste is minimized for every action. Actions that do not add value to the customer are considered as waste. Nine variations of waste can occur:

- **Overproduction**: Processing more than needed or processing too early.
- **Motion/Transportation**: Moving items farther than what is minimally required.
- **Waiting**: Items queuing to go to the next process step and people waiting for work to do.

- **Inventory**: Having more inventory than what is minimally required.
- **Extra processing**: Related to stand-alone processes that are not linked to upstream or downstream processes (e.g., inspection).
- **Defects**: The effort involved in inspecting for and fixing defects.
- **Underutilized people/resources**: The people of an organization are key assets for any firm, and in many organizations people's skill sets are not properly matched to their jobs.

Determining these types of waste is called the "minimizing waste technique." The following table might help to determine waste and to provide solutions.

	Lean	As-Is	To-Be	
Type of Waste	Concept	Current Situation	Proposed Solution	Expected Result
	Describe the action where the waste is found.	**Describe** what the waste looks like and how it is generated.	**Describe** an alternative for the as-is situation where less waste will be generated.	**Describe** what the outcome of the new proposed solution will look like.
Over-production				
Trans-portation				
Waiting				
Over-production				

	Lean	As-Is	To-Be	
Waiting				
Inventory				
Extra Processing				
Defects				
Underutilized people / resources				

And What is Six Sigma?

Six Sigma is about changing an organization's approach to managing quality and change by delivering customer satisfaction, eliminating variation in outputs, making data-driven, fact-based decisions, measuring inputs and not just outputs, and working across organizational boundaries. As mentioned above, it translates a real-world problem into a statistical problem, finds a statistical solution, and translates this back into the real world. Six Sigma focuses on reducing process variation to the point that no defects are produced. The methodology for this is called DMAIC, which stands for: **D**efine the issue; **M**easure the issue; **A**nalyze the root causes; **I**mprove the process; and **C**ontrol the results going forward. A second version of the methodology is called DFSS (Design for Six Sigma). DFSS is used to design new processes or products. The first three steps of DFSS are the same as in DMAIC, but instead of improving the process, the fourth step is to **D**esign the process or product, and the final step is to **V**erify that the design meets the critical-to-quality requirements. Here is how someone once captured the chain of causation for this philosophy:

- A company's survival is dependent on growing its business.
- Business growth is largely determined by customer satisfaction.
- Customer satisfaction is governed by price, quality, and delivery.
- Price, quality, and delivery are controlled by process capability.
- Process capability is limited by variation.
- Process variation leads to an increase in defects, cost, and cycle-time.
- To eliminate variation, we must apply the right knowledge.
- To apply the right knowledge, we must first acquire it.
- And that is Six Sigma.

Part of the numerical focus of Six Sigma is to understand the variation and cause of the variation in a process. Every process has multiple input factors—some are controllable and some are uncontrollable. These input factors combine to cause the output.

Figure 14: Process Black Box

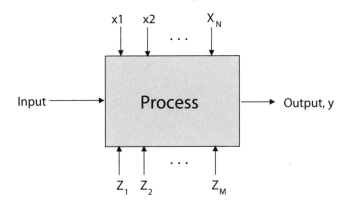

Controllable **Input Factors**

Uncontrollable **Input Factors**

Output: Y	Inputs: X1, X2, X3, . . ., Xn
Dependent	Independent
Output	Input
Effect	Cause
Symptom	Problem

So it is a fact-based methodology used to define and improve business performance using two broad methods: the Six Sigma DMAIC and the Six Sigma DMADV, each of which has five steps.

1. ***Define***—In this phase, the business problem is defined and the metrics used to measure success are established as a baseline. The focus of this phase is to really understand who the customer is. You need to look at what data has been collected for customer requirements and what the business needs to be producing in terms of products and services. This helps determine the critical dimensions of business, develop a vision for a future state of the business along these critical dimensions, and establish metrics linked to performance in each critical dimension to business improvement goals. These are called the key process output variables (KPOV) in Six Sigma terms. It's like capturing software requirements when you are starting a new project. It established the problems being addressed and the solutions being built for the same. So this builds a strategic link to business plans as defined in the project selection process. There are many Six Sigma tools used in this phase:
   - *Critical-to-quality (CTQ)*—Characteristics that significantly influence one or more of the customer requirements. CTQs are customer needs translated into critical

process requirements that are specific and measurable. A fully developed CTQ has these elements: output characteristics, target values needed, and specification/tolerance limits allowed.

- *Project charter*—This documents the vision of the project; it clarifies what is expected of the project and keeps the team focused and aligned with those organizational priorities.
- *Voice of customer (VOC)*—This defines the customer specifications or requirements that dictate acceptable and unacceptable outcomes and drive actions.
- *Voice of the process (VOP)*—This captures the company's processes and what they are doing to produce the products or services for their customers.

2. *Measure*—In this phase, current process data is gathered and measured against customer requirements. This is to understand the current performance of the process. This data collection phase establishes baseline current or as-is business performance along those critical dimensions determined in the *define* phase. It begins to establish the gaps between the current state of business and the desired state. There are many Six Sigma tools used in this phase: flow diagrams, process maps, pareto charts, priority matrices, operational definition diagrams, and, finally, quality function deployment (QFD). QFD is a tool that was developed during the 1970s in the design of an oil tanker by Mitsubishi Heavy Industries. It helps manufacturing companies design products that are not only technically elegant but also reflect customers' desires and tastes. With this tool, marketers, designers, engineers, and strategists work closely together from product conception to end result. Today QFD helps interfunctional-team conversations and is applied in a wide

variety of services, consumer products, and emerging technology products to identify and document competitive marketing strategies and tactics.

3. *Analyze*—In this phase, you begin to look at data collected to validate the base line, identify root causes of defects, and gauge the impact on the process. You begin to understand the vital inputs that go into a process and their impact on the output of the project. You begin to understand the reasons for the variation in the process and the potential causes for the same. You try to understand the root causes of the problems. There are many Six Sigma tools used in this phase: fishbone diagrams, scatter plots, regressions, and failure mode and effects analysis (FMEA). FMEA is a tool that is used to identify ways the process can fail, estimate the risk of the failure, identify causes of failure, prioritize actions to reduce failure risks, and develop control plans to prevent failures.

4. *Improve*—In this phase, you begin to outline strategies to improve key business metrics; the processes are changed to reduce variability and defect levels; and solutions are generated, tested, and selected. You develop a solution designed specifically to reduce or eliminate the impact of the root cause, as identified in the *analyze* phase, so that the process is able to meet the customer CTQs. There are many Six Sigma tools used in this phase, including design of experiments, stratification, and analysis of variance (ANOVA).

5. *Control*—In this phase, you establish metrics so as to monitor critical processes and ensure they remain effective and efficient. You begin to look at systems and structures (re-

wards, measures, staffing, training, information, etc.) that you still need to change in order to institutionalize the improvements achieved in the previous phases. Two of the Six Sigma tools used in this phase are dashboard and control charts.

As mentioned earlier, Six Sigma started in the manufacturing industry with emphasis on operational excellence, but it is being increasingly used to design new products and processes and has moved toward *customer intimacy* and *product leadership* value disciplines through its DFSS/DMADV tools, as described below. There is a debate about whether Six Sigma being so focused on end results and numbers can be stifling for innovation. But like William C. Taylor said in *Change This*,

> The most creative companies I've met don't aspire to learn from the "best in class" in their industry—especially when best in class isn't all that great. Instead, they aspire to learn from innovators far outside their industry as a way to shake things up and leapfrog the competition. Ideas that are routine in one industry can be revolutionary when they migrate to another industry, especially when those ideas challenge the prevailing assumptions that define so many industries.

And the concepts of Six Sigma can be ported to different concepts.

DMADV (define, measure, analyze, design, verify) and **IDOV** (identify, design, optimize, verify) relate to DMAIC and help close the loop on improving the end product or process during the design (DFSS) phase.

These phases parallel the four phases of the traditional Six Sigma improvement methodology, MAIC—measure, analyze, improve, and control. The similarities can be seen below.

- *Identify phase*—The identify phase tasks link the design to Voice of the Customer. This involves identifying customer and product requirements, establishing the business case, and creating a CTQ list.
- *Design phase*—The design phase tasks emphasize CTQ variables and attributes by formulating the concept design and identifying potential risks using failure modes and effects analysis (FMEA).
- *Optimize phase*—The optimize phase develops detailed design elements to predict performance and optimize design. It reassesses process capabilities to achieve critical design parameters and meet CTQ limits, and it optimizes design to minimize sensitivity of CTQs to process parameters.
- *Validate phase*—The validate phase consists of testing and validating the design and recording information for design improvements, and it does *prototype* testing and validation.

So this approach helps in new product or service development by simplifying the innovation process to improve the speed-to-market and success rate. Four questions are addressed in the innovation process: Is it a good concept? Is it realistic? Can we do it? Is it successful? By the time these questions have been answered, the emphasis moves from qualitative to financial.

Six Sigma started in the manufacturing industry with an emphasis on the management of efficient processes, efficient management of people, dedication to measurement systems, etc.—mostly *operational excellence*. But it became apparent that business success was more than the absence of negatives (such as defects, delays, or cost overruns). Sometimes you have to positively impact the products or services to get the best from a business. The outcome of such modifications to the process or the product can help with improving upon an existing product or service. In

1669, Louis XIV of France ordered that table knives have rounded, not pointed ends, to stop them being used as daggers during mealtime arguments. Just like that, Six Sigma can help encompass positives like customer loyalty and delighters in new products. From operational excellence, Six Sigma has moved toward customer intimacy and product leadership value disciplines through its DFSS/DMADV tools. Even when applied to IT, the idea is pretty simple and yet very powerful. In order to define what value is, you need to know what your business really is and what it needs (*understanding the business strategy and its alignment with IT Strategy*). And then you design a process that encourages flow and pull systems. What this means is that you need to know how much water can flow through your pipe and only put so much more through it once some has left from the other side.

> Six Sigma started in the manufacturing industry with emphasis on operational excellence, but it is being increasingly used to design new products and processes and has moved toward *customer intimacy* and *product leadership* value disciplines.

In IT management terms, you need to know your completion rate along with your lead time and project arrival rate. Once you use this information to configure an optimized service delivery organization, you have to try to take on only projects that can be handled within this pipeline. As they are executed, newer ones can be taken on. A new project enters the pipeline only after there has been one that is completed (pull system). So if you see a situation whereby there are too many business needs and all lines of business (LoBs) are screaming for resources (people, hardware, software, etc.)—like a bakery with no order number—you need to instill this discipline of establishing and managing a pipeline to handle a specific number of projects. These days CIOs also establish a portal/reporting mechanism for their internal customers to see the status of such projects (such visual boards were also used as part of the lean thinking principles in Toyota production system, [TPS]). Every CIO who I have personally worked with has asked for these mechanisms to improve internal customer satisfaction and their experience of doing business with IT. So, after the establishment and execution of these processes, customers can pull and pay for the services they need.

There is a lot of debate in the software process industry about how to apply Six Sigma principles to application development—one of the core functions in an IT organization. There were surveys done, empirical data collected, etc., in order to break the application development process into stages and try to establish correlations as below. As seen in this table below, the time to fix defects increases a lot as one moves from requirements to the released/deployed application. Ideally, the testing should be done as early as possible. That is the whole paradigm of agile methodology (as explained in chapter 4) that tries to do almost continuous testing and integration of the applications as they are being built.

Figure 15: Software Development Statistics

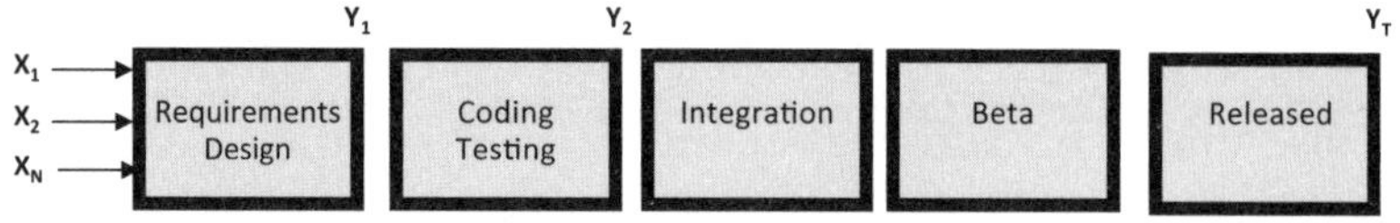

	Requirements Design	Coding Testing	Integration	Beta	Released
Defects Introduced	30%	58%	12%	0%	0%
Defects Found	7%	42%	28%	13%	10%
Time to Fix	1.2	4.9	9.5	12.1	15.3

Data Source: NIST Economic Impacts of Inadequate Sotftware Processes

Of course, we must keep in mind the story of the statistician who drowned while trying to wade across a river with an average depth of four feet, because averages hide more than they disclose. And application development is not like manufacturing anyway. In application and software development, process variation can never be eliminated because:

- No two modules are alike, and so performance includes an intrinsic degree of variability.
- There is greater variation in human cognitive processes (differences in skills from one developer to another).
- Application development processes cannot be fully characterized by three measurements that are key to establish cause-and-effect relationships:
  » *Time:* the time required to perform a task
  » *Size:* the size of the work product produced
  » *Defects:* the number and type of defects, as well as fixing time

Focus #2: Systems Capabilities

It's not easy to describe good architecture, but I'll know it when I see it.
—Someone looking at the Eiffel Tower

For every complex problem there is a simple solution that is wrong.
—George Bernard Shaw, Irish playwright and critic

In order to build anything that is a bit complex—say, a house, a building, a bridge, etc.—one needs architecture. Architecture is a model that either visualizes or provides an abstract representation of a complex idea. It acts as a bridge between vision and reality and tries to balance what's desired and what's pragmatic.

The Eiffel Tower, built as the entrance arch to the 1889 World's Fair, was one of a number of designs entered into a contest for the fair and eventually won by a company owned by Alexandre Gustav Eiffel. One of Eiffel's employees, a man named Morris Koechlin, actually designed the tower, although his first design was rejected by Eiffel. Although it was structurally sound, the design lacked "class" according to Eiffel, who considered it too plain. After Koechlin added ornate features to the design, it was approved and won the competition, and today the thousand-foot structure stands as one of the most recognizable icons of architecture in the world. Koechlin had to find a balance between what was desired and what was pragmatic, just like most IT systems need to do.

These models or abstractions, when turned into an understandable format (like blueprints), provide a plan for realizing the form, function, and use of the idea within the specified constraints (e.g., cost, resources, etc.). As Peter Senge said in his book, *The Fifth Discipline: The Art and Practice of the Learning Organization*, "When things get complicated, you can learn through analysis—breaking down the problem into digestible components. But, as things get faster and more complex still, you have to learn from dynamics—seeing how the patterns evolve over time."

For the IT organization to realistically agree to the right standards to build the system capabilities and adhere to these standards, Enterprise Architecture is a common discipline that has been adopted by many mature organizations. The definition of what it should contain is surely varied in the industry. We'll delve into the components of these systems capabilities in this chapter. But it is key to understand that even if scales (size) are different, and even if definitions are disparate, this discipline is needed to reduce costs in application development, testing costs, integration costs, and application management costs.

Eventually, as this matures across the enterprise, it leads to improved IT productivity and improved IT budget utilization. It helps improve time-to-market for new business capabilities as it helps reduce the time to build as well as deploy the system capabilities throughout the company. It leads to improved customer and partner satisfaction by improving system flexibility, scalability, simplicity, performance, interoperability, and reliability of the systems. Technology enables the applications to manage information, which allows the business to function smoothly.

Technology Architecture

This is the plumbing of the architecture. Just like pipes bringing water and electricity into a building, it includes the blueprints for defining, building, and running the IT systems' hardware. Covering all the supporting technology elements that must be present to enable and support the application layer, this includes infrastructure support and operations. Architects in this area usually specialize in a particular subject area such as hardware, system software, storage, and networking. This includes the *development architecture* that includes tools, infrastructure and processes that support new application introduction, new development, application maintenance, testing, etc. This is called the *build* environment. It also addresses the *operations architecture*, which has the components required to operate and manage the system—systems management including disaster recovery, high availability, backup/restore, performance management, etc. And lastly it should also have the *execution architecture*, which has the components required when a production application executes—staging and production infrastructure (hardware, operating system, network, middleware, web services, directory services, etc.).

Application Architecture

Applications support the business process and information, and they carry through the design and enhancement, acquisition, construction, and integration of applications.

Application architecture is the representation of the system and the functions that the software is expected to perform. Even as there are new models emerging to do applications—from the mainframe, to client server, to web or now cloud services—it is broken into layers to manage the complexity. The *user services layer* encapsulates all of the application's presentation logic, navigation, and control flow. The *business services layer* encapsulates the business logic of the application. The *data services layer* is responsible for communicating with external resources and systems, such as databases and other applications. The *business services layer* is coupled with this layer whenever the business objects require data or services that reside in an external system. The reason for this kind of segregation, as explained in the service oriented architecture section, is that the changes have less ripple effect all across the systems—change in one place does not entail change in other layers. This provides the ability for IT organizations to react faster on new business requirements and process improvements. And in the long term the industrialized IT landscape is easier to achieve—simpler systems, more flexible functionality, lower cost, and a value-driven IT footprint.

Each architectural view addresses some specific set of concerns, specific to the various stakeholders in the development process: end users, designers, developers, support personnel, etc. The goals for creating such application architecture are:

Extensibility—It is the measure of the ease (in terms of time and cost) of adding or changing features in a system. It is also a measure of the system's ability to adapt to new operating environments (software platforms, hardware platforms, external interfaces, etc.).

Scalability—It is the measure of the ability of a system to support growth. This includes the ability to process more loads (e.g., concurrent users for the application) as well as the ability to scale to store data.

Performance—It is the measure of a system's ability to perform work and includes throughput (the amount of work performed per unit time) and response time (the time required to respond to a particular event).

Availability—It is the measure of the proportion of time a system is in service (i.e., up and running). It is measured by the length of time between failures.

Security—It is the measure of a system's ability to resist unauthorized attempts at usage. It can be decomposed into the following attributes:
- Authentication—The ability to identify a user and validate "he is who he says he is." This is typically a combination of the following: what you know (e.g., a password), what you possess (e.g., a token or ID card), and who you are (e.g., fingerprint or other biometrics).

- Authorization—The ability to ensure that users can perform only those actions that they are permitted. In a role-based authentication system, users are assigned one or more predefined roles. These roles then determine what information they can see or change. For example, a manager can see the sales for the whole region, whereas the individual sales representatives can see only their sales data.

- Non-repudiation—Just like one sends registered mail, so the recipient cannot deny that a letter was delivered. In the digital world, non-repudiation is a way to guarantee that the sender of a message cannot later deny having sent the message and that the recipient cannot deny having received the message. This is done by digital signatures, etc. It is like legal documents that typically require witnesses to sign so that the person who signs cannot deny having done so.

- The application architecture is typically explained in different views so that it makes sense to all stakeholders. The *use case view* contains the use cases that encompass architecturally significant behavior. It is a subset of the use-case model. The *logical view* contains the architecturally significant design classes, their organization into subsystems, and the organization of these subsystems into layers. It is a subset of the design model. The *process view* contains a description of the tasks (processes and threads) that comprise the system, the allocation of design objects to tasks, etc. The *deployment view* contains a description of the physical environment to which the system will be deployed, including the hardware, a mapping of processes to the hardware, etc. The *implementation view* contains an overview of the organization of the implementation model.

Information Architecture

Whether a company is producing products or services, it is surely producing a lot of internal and external data to conduct its business. Information architecture deals with the way a company *stores*, *organizes*, *moves*, and *accesses* its data and information assets. The way to think of information is the classic assembly line in the manufacturing industry. Some data is received from outside the firm (suppliers), some data is produced from within, it is organized (metadata, taxonomy) for storage somewhere, and it is distributed (a.k.a. reporting, etc.) to end users (customers) for consumption. Information architecture structures data and

> Information architecture deals with the way a company *stores*, *organizes, moves*, and *accesses* its data and information assets.

data relationships to facilitate analyses that feed business strategy and optimization decisions (e.g., through data warehousing and business intelligence applications). It also serves as a foundation for application design and delivery. It is sometimes called data architecture and can include both structured and unstructured information. Bob Boiko, the chief editor of The Information Management Foundation, summed it up well by saying, "Information architecture is at the very center of the electronic information storm. Without effective means to structure and present the information we produce, we are blown about by the vast quantities and the variable quality of that information. It provides you a deep keel and a strong rudder to surf above the waves of information that buffet you." Chapter 3 discusses these capabilities in detail.

An example of this follows:

- Let's say there is a company that is a car dealer that also services cars. In order for this company to process an order, the company needs to devise its services at the level where tasks/activities are conducted (chapter 3 talks of a *process order-to-pay* process at Level 1).

This assumes that the company is focused on establishing an enterprise architecture that creates the right level of service orientation and orchestration. Service oriented architecture (SOA) is an approach to distributed computing that thinks of software resources as services available on the network. It creates an architecture that creates reusable enterprise level services that are accessible through pervasive, vendor neutral, web-based standards. Future applications "plug in" to existing services using standard technology so that integration and connectivity efforts can be reduced. Of course, the challenge is to design SOA systems with the right level of granularity of services, trading off between performance/scalability and abstraction for reuse. A solid grasp of business processes enables the IT organization to do this well.

SOA is not that different in concept from reusable application programming interfaces (API) that have been used for years. The biggest difference is that SOA leverages accepted Internet standards and protocols, which makes services much easier to share across different platforms, and these services tend to be "large grained"—they perform large chunks of functionality. For example, GoogleMaps is a large-grained web service that many retail websites invoke for directions to their stores. This new enablement of IT systems has led to a shift in the focus of IT implementations from data and partial processes to end-to-end business processes. As explained in the book *Business Process Management—The 3rd Wave* by Smith and Fingar, business process management (BPM) defines, enables, and manages the exchanges of business information on the basis of a process view that incorporates employees, customers, partners, applications, and databases. BPM products solve the problem of embedded process logic by abstracting the integration and process automation logic into a new layer of software tools. These software products liberate integration and process tasks from the underlying functional IT applications so they can be more effectively changed, managed, and optimized.

Focus #3: Organizational Capabilities—Change Enablement

Wisdom lies neither in fixity nor in change,
but in the dialectic between the two.

—Octavio Paz, Mexican poet and essayist

There is an interesting story of the Battle of Thermopylae, which was fought between some Greek states, led by King Leonidas of Sparta, and the Persian Empire of Xerxes over the course of three days, during the second Persian invasion of Greece. In this battle, a small force led by King Leonidas blocked the only road through which the massive army of Xerxes could pass. After three days of battle, a local resident named Ephialtes betrayed the Greeks by revealing a mountain path that led behind the Greek lines. Dismissing the rest of the army, King Leonidas stayed behind with three hundred Spartans and some seven hundred Thespian volunteers. The Persians succeeded in taking the pass but sustained heavy losses, extremely disproportionate to those of the Greeks. The fierce resistance of the Spartan-led army offered Athens the invaluable time to prepare for a decisive naval battle that eventually led to victory for Greece. How did Leonidas with just three hundred Spartans hold back 300,000 Persians? The secret lies in the intense training and preparation of the Spartans for war. Their numbers might have been smaller, but the capabilities of their human resources (the soldiers) were far superior. They were motivated, trained, and ready to go the extra mile. Just like then, even today sometimes small, nimble firms take away business from large, monolithic companies based on the strength of their human resources and how they construct their organization capabilities and operating models.

The key and last component of business architecture is the organization itself—its operating model and the human resources that constitute the model. This consists of culture (norms, motivations, behaviors, values, etc.), structures, teams, jobs, roles, and so on. Many organizations introducing new initiatives or undergoing transformation think that the *installation* of their new systems, processes, and/or people will mean *adoption* by the organization. They feel that the majority of the work is getting these systems and processes deployed and that will automatically lead to realization of the value targets. Most of the budgets are already consumed by this stage, anyway. And all too often, even when these initiatives (systems, processes, and tools) are properly installed, the return expected from the investments does not occur because these changes are not adopted. No one knows how to use the new systems or processes. Or the age-old resistance to change sets in.

> Many organizations introducing new initiatives or undergoing transformation think that the *installation* of their new systems, processes, and/or people will mean *adoption* by the organization.

Dysfunctional installation is about only an appearance of change, while realization is about accomplishing the substance of change—the real reason behind engaging the change effort in the first place. It is one thing to install a new CRM system for customer intimacy, but totally another to enable the internal and external sales force to use this system to offer a single view to the customer when that customer touch point happens.

The root of all change enablement lies in understanding the composition of the organization and knowing which blocks are key to achieving adoption and realization of the value goals. At the basic level, each organization is made up of hard building blocks (such as structures, policies, and work processes) and soft building blocks (people, culture, beliefs, and values). These components make up the operating model of a company, which can be further broken down into the following:

- **Functions** are the highest level of the structure and reflect the major logical groupings of services that the organization provides.
- **Services** are collections of processes that together enable the capabilities that the organization groups provide.
- **Interface points** describe how the functions of the organization, both internal and external, interact with each other.
- **Responsibilities** are the duties assigned to each function and are linked to the role descriptions of the organization.

This operating model is the blueprint of how each component within the organization functions. The leaders need to be thinking of the following questions to effect the changes they seek:

- Who are the stakeholders involved—the sponsors, change agents, targets, and customers?
- Who owns the change management responsibilities within different programs?
- How are the different change management streams inter-faced—value management, demand management, resource management, and release management?
- Are changes assessed on the value they will deliver to the business prior to their approval?
- How are associated risks assessed and communicated?
- Is there appropriate infrastructure in place to manage change-related activities such as training, communication planning, etc.?
- How is resistance to internal and external changes managed within the organization and its business units?

All too often, executives feel like they have determined the right course of action for their organization, but then something happens after the decision was made. The intended outcome never occurs. What is behind this gap between approval to move forward and failed expectations? The answer lies in the human landscape. Industry leaders have identified some of the most common reasons for the high failure rate in adoption of the change management.

The Improvement Paradox

Many improvement initiatives rely on employees who perform the day-to-day work to both guide the improvement program and make the actual improvements. It takes time for improvements to emerge; they are not instantaneous. Therefore, the first effect of an increase in improvement effort is the reduction in time an employee can allocate to existing duties. In other words, the short-term effect of an improvement effort is a decline in output or performance. As a direct result of this "air pocket," the pressure to work harder increases. The employees are then forced to cut back the time devoted to the improvement effort. This gets output and performance back on track but impedes the improvement effort. "Common sense" efforts to mitigate this effect (such as more training, new tools, or frequent communication) serve to exacerbate the problem. As Albert Einstein once observed, "Common sense is the collection of prejudices acquired by age eighteen." Sometimes "common sense" must be put aside and real-life experience put to work.

The Vision Trap

The design and execution of the program should be performed while always tracking to the overall organizational performance goals. Yet maximizing the performance of processes is invariably confused with maximizing the performance of the overall organization. Optimizing each process independently, in general, will not lead to an increased optimization for the overall organization. Ignoring the interactions between processes impedes improvement. Managing program level interdependencies is one of the most important tasks for the leaders of a change initiative.

Managing program level interdependencies is one of the most important tasks for the leaders of a change initiative.

The Tool Trap

Although tools offer very useful help to an organization, they require the development of knowledge and experience. Resource-constrained organizations unwittingly lower productivity in the short run. The increase in workload from training, learning, and practice time pushes the organization over its tipping point.

The Firefighter Trap

When an organization rewards managers for excellence in firefighting, they unwittingly create a dynamic harming the long-term performance of the organization. The long-term performance is improved by not rewarding excellence in firefighting—prevention is better than cure.

The Capability Trap

By pressuring staff to work harder, organizations unwittingly force a scenario where ever increasing levels of effort are required to maintain the same performance. Internal competition for scarce operating resources acts as a catalyst for unexpected personal, business unit, and cultural conflict. Conflicts delay decision making and the organization must work harder to maintain day-to-day performance while already stretched thin from the change effort.

As Jack Welch said, "If you are doing business now the same way you did it five years ago, it's probably obsolete." Examples of major and minor changes in every industry, every company, and every economy are all around us: fiber optics from copper, microbreweries from Budweiser, tubes versus transistors and chips, and on and on.

In psychiatric circles, counselors will tell you that one of the greatest challenges facing patients is not that they don't want to change; it's that they are fearful of it. The common saying for this is, "The certainty of misery is better than the uncertainty of change." When individuals and groups are affected by a change, they react in one of two ways: compliance or resistance. In most instances, resistance is a normal behavior and reflects an individual or group's need for control and predictability. Even when change is beneficial, the initial reaction can be one of skepticism.

> In most instances, resistance is a normal behavior and reflects an individual or group's need for control and predictability.

Resistance shows up in different ways including excessive questioning, playing devil's advocate, expressions of confusion, cynicism, or even lowered productivity.

Teambuilding, Inc., the nation's largest team-building organization, discusses this resistance in an article by Peter Grazier on their website, www.teambuildinginc.com:

> Most humans will not change their beliefs, habits, or behaviors unless they are motivated to do so. Most will not change, even if change is for the better, unless there is some compelling reason. As long as the perceived rewards of staying as we are remain greater than the rewards of changing, we will likely stay as we are. Or, conversely, as long as the perceived risks of changing are greater than the risks for staying the same, we will be unlikely to change.

As a sponsor or change leader, the key to overcoming resistance is to apply the right type of support at the right time. Change management and change enablement should use behavioral science to address the human and cultural aspects of introducing important changes (developing commitment, minimizing resistance, fostering resilience, etc.) within organizational settings. The Resistance Triangle, as shown below, is a helpful model for understanding resistance and the type of support required for each level in the triangle. The three levels described in the Resistance Triangle are information, education, and motivation.

Figure 16: Enabling Change Management

WILLING
Institutionalize

ABLE
Educate

KNOW
Inform

Get to the root of the resistance

1. **Communicate information (KNOW):** The employees need to know the who, what, when, where, and why of the change.
2. **Provide education (ABLE):** Employees learn how to operate successfully in the new environment. This includes training, communication programs, town halls, etc.
3. **Encourage motivation (WILLING):** This involves building the right rewards, incentives, and feedback to institutionalize the changes.

When Alan Mulally became boss of an ailing Ford Motor Company in 2006, one of the first things he did was demand that his executives own up to the areas in need of improvement. He asked managers to color code their progress reports—ranging from green for good to red for trouble. At one early meeting he expressed astonishment at being confronted by a sea of green, even though the company had lost several billion dollars in the previous year. Ford's recovery began only when he got his managers to admit that things weren't entirely green.

As enablers of the change, leaders will need to assess groups and individuals to determine where they are on the Resistance Triangle and determine what interventions are needed to support employees to fully adopt the change. Culture assessment and impact analysis are critical elements in assessing the current state and preparing the organization for change in the future state. So one of the first steps in a change effort is to develop a clear snapshot of what the future will look like for the division or organization when the change is implemented. This is the future state that the company is striving to put in place. The data gathered will enable the leaders to make a cultural comparison between current and future states to understand what kind of behavioral, structural, and operational changes need to occur.

The cultural assessment will help gauge the high-level organizational capacity to change. This component estimates, at a high level, the relative ease or difficulty that the sponsoring organization would have in initiating and/or sustaining a change program. The sponsoring organization's perceptions, along with the team's observations of relative willingness, readiness, and ability to change, formulate the high-level estimation. It has been clearly established that information on "who" or "what/why" can help drive change (people, roles, groups, outside events, etc.). And when people do not understand the "who" and "what/why" of the changes being established, their natural reaction is to resist the change. The qualitative descriptions and frequency of mentions also help in the awareness and acceptance of change.

The impact analysis is often done at multiple points in the project to maintain a clear picture of how the change will impact the business. It is an audit that helps clarify the types of impacts the change will create throughout the organization. This focuses on business and organizational impact such as management systems, processes, technology, and equipment changes. It also looks at personal and cultural impacts such as employee mindset, employee recognition, and team effectiveness. It is a powerful tool to expand the leadership's understanding of the breadth and depth of the changes required for successful realization of goals.

Stakeholder Analysis

The stakeholder analysis is an important exercise that enables project leadership to identify everyone who has a stake in the change effort, whether a leader of the change, someone who is impacted significantly by the change, or someone who is implementing the change. The plan provides a useful reference for evaluating stakeholder needs as the change strategy and implementation plan are taking shape. A map or list of all stakeholders should be constructed, and each stakeholder should be evaluated in terms of the level of awareness and support he or she currently has. One needs to identify groups who will be directly or indirectly *affected by* the change and those that will be *effecting* the change. Specific communication and involvement strategies should be put in place to ensure that all stakeholder groups have the required information, support, and reinforcement that will enable them to fully support the change.

Information gathered from the stakeholder analysis informs the change management plan as it is developed. This includes talking to sponsors who had initiated the change, the sponsors who will sustain and experience the change (sometimes they are different sets of people), the change agents, the advocates, the influencers, and the information partners. And then you need to determine potential barriers and enablers of change for these stakeholders. These could include change roles, communication, capabilities, commitments/priorities, or simple resistance culture. A sample data capture of this exercise is shown below:

Stake-Holder	Level of Awareness (1-5)	Level of Support (1-5)	Desired Level of Awareness/Support	Mitigating Strategies
Joe Smith	2	2	4	Presentation at team meeting

Readiness Assessment

A thorough readiness assessment enables leadership and key stakeholders to understand the level of receptivity and readiness to support the change. Readiness questions fall into roughly seven areas of the project: change leadership, need for the change, vision for the change, key relationships, structure/management practices/rewards, project execution/learning, and lessons learned.

Some sample readiness questions:

Challenge Area	Sample Question	Required Action
Change Leadership	Is there clear ownership and a mandate for the change from sponsors?	
Need for Change	Has the case for change been clearly articulated and widely disseminated?	

Challenge Area	Sample Question	Required Action
Change Vision	Can we concisely, compellingly, and consistently describe the desired outcomes?	
Relationships	Have we identified all stakeholders necessary for success?	
Structure, Management Practices, Rewards	Does the organization have the right skills and abilities to achieve results?	
Project Execution	Do we have timely, visible measures for tracking our progress and results?	
Lessons Learned	Have we identified relevant learning from previous successes and failures and are we applying it to this project?	

Information gathered in the readiness assessment exercise should be used to create the adequate artifacts that help navigate the change management activities:

Change Assessment • Who needs to change? Which organizations? • What are internal capabilities to support the change?	• Stakeholder maps showing who, where, and when

Understand Change • Why is this change necessary? • What will the change look like? • How will this change occur? • When will the change occur?	• Case for action • Description of the new business model • A project road map • Communication strategy and plan
Embrace Change • Who is involved in the change from my area? • How will this change specifically affect me? • How will I be rewarded for the change? • How can I be involved in the implementation?	• New organizational models, job descriptions • Pay/reward system review • Participation programs to be a part of the change
Enable Change • Who will be managing the change? • What are the new skills I will need to carry out change? • How will I acquire these skills? • How will I be transitioned to my new job?	• Governance structure/ program • Education and training programs • Transition programs

Hence, there is more to change management than just communication and learning. Successful implementation programs must address comprehensive change agenda needs across five key areas: communication, learning and training, ownership and sponsorship, organizational changes and performance management, and business readiness and measurement.

A combination of communication events including presentations, meetings, and town hall meetings can be used to build awareness and interest, disseminate information, and keep employees and teams updated throughout the project life. Communicating the correct message is key. We all have heard a hilarious story of the new guy, in this case a director for a business unit of a company in Sydney, Australia. As with any new employee, he's eager to make an impact. His boss says that the sales team is meeting in Jervis Bay (a coastal holiday spot about a three-hour drive from Sydney) on Monday morning at 9:00 a.m. Mike gets up at 4:00 a.m. on Monday and drives down to Jervis Bay and on arrival calls his boss to get the specific location of the meeting. After getting the call the boss says, "No, no, we are meeting in the Sydney office in a meeting room called Jervis Bay." Miscommunication is worse than the lack of it in some ways.

Begin communicating with stakeholders at the outset of the program and continue at regular intervals throughout the program's execution. Early points of communication typically include communication of program expectations and requirements, communication of key strategies and program plans, and communication of initial and revised detailed plans regarding upcoming mobilization and execution activities. Effective communication management with stakeholders facilitates the change process by:

- Reinforcing the vision and enhancing understanding of the program
- Promoting acceptance and ownership of the program by the sponsoring organization management and workforce

- Improving morale during times of change by establishing an environment of cooperation
- Increasing the integrity and accuracy of information being transmitted within the organization

To obtain these objectives, a communications plan should be developed that includes clear and specific objectives, identifies the various audiences, and analyzes their communication needs. It should assess effective and ineffective channels of communication for the messages and audiences.

The change management approach entails several key change process components and steps that will be fully integrated within the program. The change components ensure a full understanding of the change risks and organizational readiness, cultural challenges and impact of the change, stakeholder analysis, and a fully developed change management plan that will address the communication, learning, and sustainment steps and activities.

Industry experience indicates that on average, only about 30 percent of change initiatives achieve their full intended benefit. The focus must be on delivering "real" change, which will require more than the installation of new processes or the rollout of new taglines or slogans. In order to realize the full intended benefit of the change, attention must not only be on *what* strategy or solution to implement but also *how* to implement the solution well in order to realize the promised benefit. Full realization requires full engagement of leaders, understanding of the potential barriers to change, a well-thought-out change strategy, and rigorous attention to managing the change process and the human dynamics of change. An implementation strategy must be in place to ensure barriers to change—such as

> The focus must be on delivering "real" change, which will require more than the installation of new processes or the rollout of new taglines or slogans.

resistance, leadership, capacity, alignment, and culture—are overcome and a solution is reached.

> A rigorous approach to change requires an integrated effort between the three key components of the change effort: content, process, and people.

A rigorous approach to change requires an integrated effort between the three key components of the change effort: content, process, and people. Content entails the content of the change itself or the changes that are implemented to move from the current state to a future state. Process includes the implementation strategy and project plan. The people component includes the elements that represent the biggest potential barriers to success. These include resistance to change, ability to effect culture change, employees' capacity for change, and leadership commitment to the change effort.

Based on the maturity of the organization's operating model and the impact of forthcoming changes, it is important to determine a set of *change enablement* activities that are employed to manage and sustain the organization. It is very critical that the leaders clarify and communicate the business drivers, key imperatives, and sense of urgency that support the initiative. They should work toward providing end users with the critical knowledge, skills, processes, and tools that enable them to succeed in the new environment. The leadership team should coach and empower resources to take action and make the change effort successful. There needs to be a plan for moving the current organization to the desired future state. Typical components of the change plan include the following:

- *Job design:* Ensures realignment of roles and responsibilities with new workflows, organization sizing, and alignment of reporting structures with new workflows.
- *Performance management:* Ensures that individual performance measures are aligned with new processes and business goals.

- *Training:* Supports acquiring new knowledge and building new skills. There needs to be a focus on who will perform documentation and delivery of the training deliverables.
- *Performance support:* Provides timely post-implementation guidance and knowledge. How are measures identified and implemented?
- *Communication and sponsorship:* Delivers key program messages to create awareness, demonstrates senior executive support and buy-in, and provides the opportunity for ownership and involvement. How many communication events are anticipated and across what types of media? Who creates materials and drives delivery of the communication plan?

Organizational Capabilities— Knowledge Management

As the world becomes more interconnected,
and business becomes more complex and dynamic . . .
organizations that will truly excel in the future will be those
that discover how to tap people's commitment and capacity
to learn at all levels in the organization.
—Peter Senge, *The Fifth Discipline*

If a little knowledge is dangerous, where
is the man who has so much as to be out of danger?
—Thomas Henry Huxley, English biologist known as "Darwin's Bulldog"

Thomas H. Davenport said in *The McKinsey Quarterly* (2011),

The problems of free access are fairly obvious: while workers may know how to use technology tools, they may not be skilled at searching for, using, or sharing the knowledge. One survey revealed that over a quarter of a typical knowledge worker's time is spent searching for information. Another found that only 16 percent of the content within typical businesses is posted to locations where other workers can access it. Most knowledge workers haven't been trained in search or knowledge management and have an incomplete understanding of how to use data sources and analytical tools.

Depending on the company-specific profit drivers and value structure (the primary types of assets that drive value, such as intellectual property or physical assets), as well as the level of change within the industry, there is more and more focus on building

115

knowledge management (KM) capabilities. The evolution of this important discipline has been as below:

Figure 17: Evolution of Knowledge Management

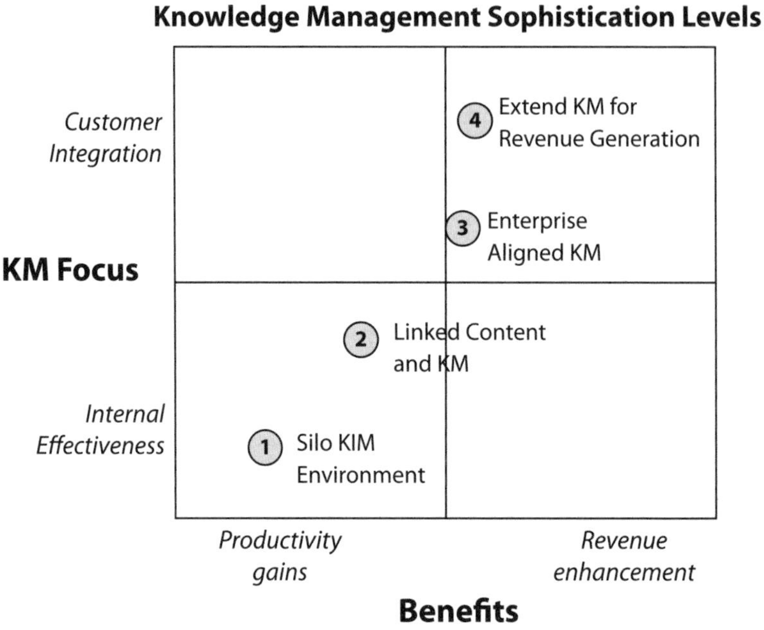

Knowledge Management Sophistication Levels

1. **Silo KM Environment**—The knowledge captured is grouped and used in organizational silos, and there is limited or opportunistic usage of this capital.
2. **Linked Content KM**—At this level of maturity the organization has some formal knowledge and content management processes within practice silos at a broader organizational level. However, there is limited access to this knowledge, and there is a need to have common tools to access information and categorize them.
3. **Aligned KM**—This has the beginnings of enterprise knowledge management with aligned governance for the same. KM metrics are established for creation, utilization, and

trending of the knowledge assets within the organization. This involves multiple, integrated channels of KM (e.g., business intelligence for Insurance, master data management for the back office supply chain processes, etc.).

4. *Extended KM*—The company starts to look at commercialization of IP assets (e.g., automated scorecard generator, etc.). There are the beginnings of formal IP (e.g., life insurance claims processes automated, etc.).

Framework for Knowledge Management

The following considerations are important to design an effective KM discipline within the organization:

Knowledge Strategy, Organization, and Governance

- What data, information, and knowledge is critical to capture?
- What is currently available? Where are there gaps? How are these to be filled?
- Should *communities of practice* be organized? Other forms of collaboration?
- How should information be presented to be effective?

Content and Intellectual Property (IP) Management

- Who "owns" the content?
- How is IP being identified?
- How is content usage encouraged or ensured?

Collaboration and Network Management

- What communities or subject matter expert (SME) practices should be created?
- How should these operate and how should they be managed—practice areas or regional branches?
- Who would participate and who would facilitate?

Content Storage and Architecture

- How should the content be organized so it can be easily found and retrieved?
- How should content be stored?
- How are content items linked to each other?
- Who "owns" it for maintenance?

Measurements, Incentives, and Operations

- What would constitute success and how will it be measured?
- What are incentives for the practitioners?
- Where does it report in the organization?

Technology and Workspace Portals

- What are the technologies that will be used—collaboration portals, search engines, discussion forums, webcasts, etc.?

IT Spend

It is not the horse that draws the cart, but the oats.
—Assyrian Proverb

In my discussions with the executive teams in companies, I hear that despite economic downturns (like in 2008), their IT organizations are thinking of spending some of their budget on innovative initiatives, so that when we get to the bottom of the J-curve in the economy, they'll be ready to win over strategic goals. Makes you wonder—how are companies dividing their IT spend on keep-the-lights-on operations and strategic or innovative investment?

Of course, a company's position on its spending is dependent upon many macro factors like number and size of competitors, industry growth rate, rate of change, industry margins/pricing, and product differentiation factors—physical products or knowledge assets. Several major factors, common across both public and commercial sectors, have contributed to an increased focus on IT spend analyses, including:

- Many years of distributed IS/IT spending and investment within specific functions and/or organization boundaries (no enterprise-wide investment management process)
- Increased cost pressure and desire to improve the synergy of IS/IT investments across organization boundaries (eliminate redundant vendor and technology investments, consolidate IT assets)
- A growing need to integrate infrastructure and enterprise solutions across external customers, suppliers, and partners
- Significant merger/integration activity to achieve economies of scale and remain competitive

- Growing demands from the business to increase the strategic utilization of information technology and produce greater impact from the existing levels of IS/IT investment
- The typical IT spend across industries reveals:
  » The average company spends about 4 percent of gross revenue on IT.
  » The industries that spend the most on IT are financial services, IT, and telecommunications.
  » The typical firm spends about $6,000 to $7,000 per year per employee on IT.
  » IT head count comprises 5 to 7 percent of the total employee population in the typical enterprise.

Working in combination, these major factors have often resulted in suboptimal IT spending over the years. In many cases, the majority of the annual IT budget is allocated to maintenance and sustaining activities rather than strategic or new capabilities impacting the current priorities of the business. I guess it's always important for the IT organization to evaluate internally how IT's value contribution to the business should be planned, managed, and assessed. Unfortunately, executives do not often understand the link between business value and IT, especially in times like these IT spending levels are overly-squeezed. IT spending level is based on historical or competitive benchmark levels. There is also a lack of recognition for IT contribution on the business side.

In the short term, simple IT cost cutting drives down value-adding and innovative IT initiatives first. As a result, IT capabilities deteriorate and midterm IT operating costs rise. Eventually, higher IT operating costs eat away funds for innovations, and this furthers the overall IT budget explosion. A big vicious circle! As the Merriam-Webster dictionary defines the term *vicious circle*: "A chain of events in which the response to one difficulty creates a new problem that aggravates the original difficulty." The origins of the term date back to the eighteenth century; in 1792 it appeared in the third edition of *The Encyclopedia Britannica.* Logicians of the era used it to define a fallacious proof in which A depends on B, B depends on C, and C in turn depends upon A. A vicious circle, indeed! In this type of pattern, whether in IT or elsewhere in life, active steps must be taken to break the cycle and begin a new pattern. And the key is to start understanding where the IT organization spends budgets and whether it is on capability building or just operations.

> The key is to start understanding where the IT organization spends budgets and whether it is on capability building or just operations.

Mandatory or nondiscretionary IT investments are for keep-the-lights-on functions—IT operations, regulatory and compliance requirements, mandatory projects and maintenance, etc. Things like technical support, IT infrastructure management (for email, websites, applications, etc.), technical upgrades to infrastructure components, software upgrades, or required and scheduled maintenance all fall in this category. Discretionary spending, which is about IT investments that are strategic, enabling, and sustaining, is on things like R&D (focus on future technologies), new workflows, analytics, and web page changes. These are business-driven projects that enhance applications or develop infrastructure. These investments should create a strategic or economic advantage in the market place, create barriers to entry, and so on. Depending on the rate of change in the industry of a company, these kinds of value creation budget items should have at least 35 to 40 percent of the budget for a leading organization. But in many organizations the nondiscretionary bucket consumes 70 to 90 percent of the IT budget. There is a mandatory spend for the IT organization to keep the lights of the business on—this includes compliance issues, plumbing maintenance (emails, networks, etc.), preventative maintenance (end-of-life software and hardware), and corrective fixes.

As written by Michael Treacy and Fred Wiersema in their classic book, *Discipline of Market Leaders*, there are three basic "value disciplines" for a company to pursue—operational excellence, customer intimacy, and/or product leadership. If the direction of the company is clear, well communicated, and well understood, then some strategic IT investments are driven from the same disciplines:

If there is a *product/service innovation* focus, then the company needs to focus on increasing value to existing customers, developing new markets and channels, etc. Examples of initiatives are e-innovation, e-design collaboration, and product lifecycle management (PLM).

If the company is focusing on *customer intimacy*, then the company needs to improve understanding of its customer needs, increase customer insight, etc. The initiatives fall in realms like customer insight (inbound marketing), and integrated view of customer (data warehouse [DW], analytics).

If the company is trying to *create new scales and reduce interaction costs* between partners and customers, it needs to invest in increasing service levels at lower costs through concepts like "super" distributor, supplier collaboration, etc.

There are several frameworks, and they are not mutually exclusive, but understanding the way to analyze and report IT expenditure can help focus the correct data gathering and drive the structure of the IT cost model. There are various frameworks for categorizing the different IT expenditure:

- ***IT organization or cost center:*** IT costs are categorized by cost center within the IT organization. This is the most frequently used native model because it is aligned with the way budgets are defined. The organization costs can be broken down into several categories, like service delivery, service management, front and back office solutions, and application maintenance.

- *IT operating model:* This looks across organizational boundaries to develop costs for functions (e.g., project management [PM], app delivery, IT admin). This is typically a very helpful view for IT transformation. Typically companies will categorize the spending into buckets like service management, service integration, solution development, service delivery, IT planning and management, etc.
- *Business operating model:* IT costs directly enabling each source of value added in the business; may focus on application and mapped infrastructure assets enabling the business. The categories for IT spending can be sourcing, making, selling, servicing, and the general enterprise support functions like HR, finance, etc.
- *IT service catalog:* Economics of the product and services delivered (cost to serve) include the fixed and variable IT costs and the economic drivers (e.g., service levels, number of servers, number of calls, etc.). The broad categories of spending are hardware (network, workstations, computing, storage, etc.), software (operating systems, databases, etc.), facilities, internal labor, and external professional services costs.

Building a Detailed Business Case

Business cases highlight the initiatives that create the greatest value, support decision making, and help track program performance. It is good to define the business case early and plan on many iterations, since it demonstrates how a major investment creates value and typically includes both quantitative and qualitative rationale. They should have benefit models, cost models, cash flow models, assumptions (timing, dependencies), sensitivity analyses, and also a qualitative factors analysis (nonfinancial benefits and risks). This exhaustive approach supports business decisions by weighing choices or options, creates a way to track performance and measure success after a decision has been made, and gains alignment and management consensus for a project. In some organizations, the term "business case" may also be referred to as cost/benefit analysis, ROI analysis, feasibility study, or capital funding request.

A "business case" has three purposes. The first is to understand value by identifying the value levers and quantifying the value that the initiative will provide. The second is to support decisions by quantifying impact and doing sensitivity analyses on the same. The third purpose is to track performance by measuring the existing baseline and the successful impact, and adjusting actions accordingly.

Even when the importance of having a business case is established, companies struggle with the level of detail that should go into one. The financial models can be *top down* (more high level and helps form an initial hypothesis with wider ranges to reflect uncertainty) or *bottom up* (more quantitative, with time spent on thorough data collection and analyses). But the key point is that you need to build the business case with ranges and confidence levels. Once the numbers are compelling, the ranges could change, but they would not change the decision or direction. As President Harry Truman joked once, when tired of conflicting views from economists, "All my economists say, 'on one hand . . . on the other.' Give me a one-handed economist!"

> The key point is that you need to build the business case with ranges and confidence levels. Once the numbers are compelling, the ranges could change, but they would not change the decision or direction.

An example of a business case structure is as below:

I. Executive Summary

II. Detailed Sections

1. Initiative Description
    - Overview of the program
    - Business needs/imperatives addressed
    - High-level business value delivered or enabled

2. Financial Analysis (return on investment [ROI], net present value [NPV], payback period)
    - Benefits
        - Hard (e.g., cost reduction, cost avoidance, revenue enhancements, etc.)
        - Soft (e.g., operational efficiency, risk mitigation, capability improvement)
    - Costs (hardware [HW], software [SW], labor)
        - One-time
        - Recurring
    - Assumptions (e.g., labor mix, labor rates, etc.)

3. Financial Summary by value levers
    - Categorize benefits/costs along business dimensions

4. Risk/issues and mitigation plans
    - Business risk
    - Technology risk
    - Financial risk
    - Management risk
    - Schedule risk

III. Appendices

1. IT baseline over targeted time horizon

2. Options considered for each program
    - Technology solutions
    - Sourcing alternatives

Process for developing a detailed business case:

Step 1: Determine Approach

It is very important to understand clearly the overall purpose of the business case. It could be to justify an investment, or determine the optimal course of action or decision, or support a case for change, or merely to provide input into a budget or financial plan. After this you need to determine what critical pieces of information must the business case convey to support the overall purpose:

> It is very important to understand clearly the overall purpose of the business case.

- Magnitude and timing of the benefits
- Magnitude and timing of the investments and costs
- Financial metrics the decision makers are looking for—net present value (NPV), internal rate of return (IRR), payback period, or ROI

The approach of almost any business case is to show the baseline of value and then show the differential value that a particular initiative has.

$$V_{company} = V_{today} + \Delta V_{initiative}$$

The value of the company = as-is company value (without changes) + *incremental* value originated by the change program. The baseline depicts the business outcome of the current state ("as-is") business condition (i.e., without making an investment). This baseline acts as a common reference frame that is used to compare the performance of each alternate future state scenario. These future scenarios depict possible future state ("to-be") conditions resulting from pursuing a particular option or an investment choice. Especially when the company is doing a program that has many interdependencies between projects, an accurate baseline needs to be in place before receiving "future state" financial and asset information back from the individual projects. A senior program manager once claimed, "I am the program manager of a $15 million initiative to redo our CRM systems. And I have only four direct reports. I am utilizing resources from all business units and it creates resource conflicts. Sometimes they contradict each other in terms of policies, procedures, or organization. And they compete for the same limited pool of available funds." Some good practices when establishing baselines:

- Create the most realistic baseline possible.
- Avoid temptation to assume a flat baseline—if costs or revenues are anticipated to increase or decline, reflect this in the baseline scenario. Also project the anticipated growth that the organization will be seeing anyway as part of its natural course (e.g., in many organizations storage needs increase at a steady rate every year).
- Carefully consider the possible impact of initiatives that the client is currently undertaking or plans to undertake that may affect the baseline or benefit calculation.
- Attempt to align the baseline with the company's financial or operating budget or budgeting process so that it will be easy to tie back to the results of the business case.

Step 2: Develop and Document Assumptions

Assumptions around certain inputs should be documented explicitly—cost of capital, discount rate, start year for benefits/costs, marginal tax rate, expected revenue growth, etc. These stipulate the scope and boundaries of the analysis and convey what data is included or excluded. Assumptions must be explicitly called out since they generally require business judgment and/or may not be obvious to the audience. Assumptions simplify business case inputs

> Assumptions around certain inputs should be documented explicitly.

so that they are easier to manage and help forecast business case inputs that could change. The assumptions elements include:

- *Time*—The total period covered in the analysis (e.g., next eighteen months, next five years), beginning and ending points for the analysis (e.g., starting Q4'02, ending Q4'05), as well as clarification of time period details (e.g., calendar years, fiscal years, quarters, etc.).

- *Geography/location*—Geographies or regions included in the analysis (e.g., United States only, North America only, worldwide, etc.). It is good to mention the specific facilities or operations included in the analyses (e.g., manufacturing facilities only, manufacturing and distribution facilities only, data centers only or co-locations as well, etc.).

- *Organization/function*—It is important to state the organizations involved (e.g., one division vs. entire company), functions involved (e.g., sales and marketing group, HR, IT, finance and accounting, etc.), as well as levels of human resources (e.g., hourly labor, management, contractors, etc.).

An illustration of assumptions for a data center consolidation program could be as follows:

- **Program Level Assumptions**
  - Initial migration into the new data center will begin in <<date>>.
- **Global Assumptions**
  - Tax Rate: 9.25%
  - Discount Rate for NPV: 12.3%
- **Server Asset Assumptions**
  - Refresh Rate (years): 3
  - Server Depreciation Rate (years): 3
  - Rack Depreciation Rate (years): 3

- Server Counts (as of <<date>>):
- Server Growth (annual): 5%
- Servers per Rack: 32
- HW Maintenance Cost: $1,200/server
- SW Maintenance Cost: $590/server
- **Storage Asset Assumptions**
  - Storage Cost per TB: $32,020 (includes rack costs)
  - Warranty Period (months): 36
  - Refreshment Cycle (months): 48
  - Storage Depreciation Rate (months): 12

Step 3: Determine Benefits

Determining and making reasonable assumptions around the timing and magnitude of benefits is the most debated section of the business case. An operations SVP of a Fortune 100 company once described his dilemma:

> We are implementing an e-invoicing and e-procurement solution with some of our easy supplier targets and in parallel moving to intelligent data capture. The speed at which the project moves is directly related to that amount of resource committed to it from our IT team and there is no hard and fast rule as to how quickly 100 percent (or near to it) can be achieved.

There are typically two approaches to building the business with its costs and benefits:

- **Top down approach**—Benefits are determined though use of macro-level data and macro-level assumptions. In this approach there is typically a case built by analogy or comparison and the range of benefits used reflect a high degree of uncertainty. This approach is generally utilized when detailed data is not readily available or a detailed business case is not possible.

- **Bottom up approach**—In this approach, benefits are determined through improvements in business process metrics. Generally, this requires more data collection and time but makes the analyses more credible and tangible.

If possible, one should attempt to isolate benefits and costs associated with the technology change versus the people and process changes. What happens in large and small programs is that the different teams that compose process work or systems work will show benefits due to their work stream. The goal is to avoid double counting and redundancy. One program manager said, "That's what I have to do all day every day to make sure the benefits we signed up for can be realized. As long as the whole orchestra is humming to good overall music, we are in good shape." All benefits are captured by the project, but some benefits are specific to people and process changes versus benefits specific to technology changes. Initial benefits can be achieved with changes to people and processes only, but they may require technology changes to remain sustainable over the long term. In either case, benefits can be categorized as one of the following:

> If possible, one should attempt to isolate benefits and costs associated with the technology change versus the people and process changes.

- *Hard benefits*—This includes areas of revenue enhancement (like market share increase, volume of sales increase, price–product optimization, etc.), cost reduction/cost elimination, and increased capital efficiency.
- *Soft benefits*—This includes areas that cannot be easily quantified, such as risk mitigation capability improvement.

As an example, data center consolidation can provide *cost reduction* by reducing the number of locations, thereby eliminating facilities costs and increasing economics of scale for location-intensive activities such as management and security. It can also provide *operational efficiency* as deployment of new servers and storage is streamlined and provisioning and installation is simplified. Operations will be harmonized—avoiding future costs due to the establishment of standards—and there will be greater capacity for scalable growth. This also offers mitigation of business risk by having appropriate mission critical facilities, thereby improving disaster recovery and business continuity planning. Choosing specific locations will also reduce the probability of risk and disaster overall. All of this will also provide *capability improvement* by increasing agility—enabling faster time-to-market for business-critical applications and modularizing services to businesses at various levels, such as storage, computing, databases, etc.

Step 4: Determine Costs
This includes the recurring and one-time costs, and the categorization depends on the accounting policies of a company:

- *Operating Expenses*—This typically includes income statement items like internal labor costs, third-party labor costs, travel, supplies, etc.; cash outflows from initial implementation-related expenses and ongoing operating expenses in the future state scenario; and nondepreciated items like labor.

- *Capital Expenditures*—This is the cash outflow for asset purchases during initial implementation and on an ongoing basis in the future state scenario. These are typically balance sheet items that are depreciated or amortized like hardware (servers, PCs/workstations, storage, networking/communications, etc.) or software (application software, database software, development/middleware/integration software, systems management software, etc.).

Step 5: Calculate Financial Impact

This step involves converting the scenario's benefits and costs into incremental cash inflows and cash outflows, laying out cash inflows and cash outflows over time, and determining the net cash flows over time. This calculates key metrics such as net present value (NPV), internal rate of return (IRR), and payback period, and when "full value" analyses are performed, then ROIC and EVA can be calculated.

Step 6: Perform Sensitivity Analyses

Sensitivity analysis is an important part of the business case because it demonstrates how changes in assumptions affect the financial results. A simple sensitivity analysis is performed by changing the values of one or more input assumptions and observing the effects on the financial results (e.g., changes to NPV, IRR, and/or payback period). Some inputs when modified slightly might cause the financial results to change dramatically. Special attention must be placed on these highly sensitive assumptions, since they have can have a significant impact on the overall business case.

Step 7: Perform Risk Analyses

Risk analysis involves evaluating the likelihood of achieving the predicted financial results. There are many advanced risk analyses that involve determining the likelihood or probability that input values and assumptions will change from an expected value. A statistical simulation (e.g., Monte Carlo) is then used to determine the expected value of the financial result (e.g., cash flows or NPV) based on the probability distribution of the input values. Sometimes, for high-level risk impact considerations, the financial models either increase the discount rate or reduce expected cash flows by a scaling factor. Several types of risk could affect the financial results, depending upon the client situation and the type of investment being considered.

- *Business risk*: This type of risk is induced if the project delivery has some impact on operations/business continuity. This includes market risk, regulatory risk, and competitive reaction risk.
- *Technology risk:* This type of risk is induced if there is use of technology that is not mature or stable (i.e., new or leading-edge technology) or if a company does not have significant experience with this technology. This can also be induced if the complexity of integration with existing technologies is very high.
- *Financial risk:* This type of risk is induced if the size of the investment needed is big and the recoverability period is long. This includes inflationary risk, cash flow risk, and exchange rate risk.
- *Skills/management risk:* This type of risk is induced if there is limited access to the specific skills required for project delivery.
- *Schedule risk:* This type of risk is induced if other projects within the program have significant dependencies upon the project schedule.

Step 8: Summarize Findings

It is important that conclusions and recommendations need to tie back to the overall purpose of the business case. Recommendations must clearly identify and explain which scenario best achieves the business objectives. It is crucial to articulate the critical success factors and how they can be managed in order to achieve the estimated benefits (e.g., required behavior changes, process and technology changes, controls, etc.) and to highlight how changes in the assumptions would alter the business case results.

> It is important that conclusions and recommendations need to tie back to the overall purpose of the business case.

Shared Services

Over the years, many companies have created shared services to put some discipline on the spending of some business functions and the value they generate. A shared services organization operates as an independent business unit within a company that specializes in delivering high quality, low cost, and standardized service offerings with a continued focus on service orientation and customer responsiveness. More and more companies have been successfully consolidating back-office and day-to-day operations into a central unit that offers economies of scale and increases both efficiency (faster and cheaper) and effectiveness (better). Examples of areas within a firm that have these models are general accounting, cash disbursement, HR, and payroll. Depending on the operating model of a company—whether central or federated—and how the value chain is enabling creation of the customer value, lots of companies have begun to look at having IT operations under a shared services model. The shared services model combines the best of both models (centralized and federated):

- Eliminates redundancy through process and technology standardization
- Consolidates and redesigns non-core support functions into service centers
- Redesigns the retained organization and responsibilities in the operating units
- Drives shared responsibility for results using two-way service level agreements (SLAs)
- Operates like a business with high focus on client service and cost management

Steps to Creating a Shared Services Organization:

Establish Service Portfolio and Catalog
Gather requirements from customers, then decide and implement the best way to acquire talent, screen/test applicants, check backgrounds, negotiate positions, and offer relocation assistance.

Develop SLAs and Resource Allocation Targets
Define the scope of services and identify expected volumes of services that will be required by the operating units. Once that is established, some high-level allocation of costs needs to be built to establish the expected cost of the services based on volumes. Identify the performance metrics and service targets that allow shared services and its customers to measure whether expected service levels are met.

Measure and Report to Clients on SLA Commitments
On a regular basis (preferably monthly), shared services should report to its customers how the process performed versus the expected service targets. Performance versus SLAs should first be reviewed by the executives as part of their normal performance review process. SLA performance reports should then be distributed to clients along with explanations of variances. Accountability for throughput and output variances should rest with shared services functional leads.

Measure and Report on a Scorecard of Internal Performance
After doing all this to set up the right structure for a shared service organization within the company, the key is to install mechanisms to measure whether it is providing the benefits that were envisioned at the start. Key questions to ask: How will this unit measure the level of service it is delivering to its customers? How will management assess itself organizationally? Are the processes working as

intended? Will anticipated transaction volumes be met? Are shared service center employees working efficiently?

The key is to establish metrics and key performance indicators (KPIs) to establish the results. KPIs should primarily be used to determine the efficiency and effectiveness of the shared services organization, the processes it operates, and the people who perform these. KPIs allow an organization to analyze aspects of its past, challenge its present, and plan its future. These should be quantifiable measurements for evaluating progress toward an organization's goals. They should be linked to business outcomes and the critical success factors that describe the conditions when these have been achieved. KPIs typically include three components: measures—the chosen focus area for measurement; goals—the target performance associated with the measure; and accountability—the assignment of the goal to a specific individual or group.

Allocate Costs to Operating Units through a Chargeback Model

Since a shared services organization is typically a cost center and not a profit center, all costs must be allocated to the operating units. In certain cases, particularly when services are provided to outside parties, shared services can charge a margin on its costs and make a profit; otherwise, the amount charged to clients must exactly equal costs incurred. The method by which costs are charged to the operating units affects both operating unit profitability and operating unit costs. The chargeback mechanism for IT is a uniform process for the recovery of IT costs from the various business units. It provides each business unit (or business user) with a charge for IT services requested (based on the IT service catalog). It also facilitates the dialogue between the business and IT on the value of IT services (money spent on IT versus business value achieved). The

> Since a shared services organization is typically a cost center and not a profit center, all costs must be allocated to the operating units.

chargeback model can be a powerful service management tool by providing better visibility of service costs and greater transparency into all of the components that make up the service cost. It establishes a clear linkage between usage of standard and/or more cost-effective processes (e.g., usage of POs), overall processing cycle time, and costs in order to drive better behaviors. The key principles for creating the right chargeback structure are:

- *Cost recovery*—Operating as a cost center, IT will only recover actual costs incurred. IT's income from chargeback will equal its actual expenditures.

- *Based on services*—Chargeback will be based on IT services provided to the various business units.

- *Usage vs. allocation*—Chargeback will be based on actual usage of IT services as opposed to the current practice of allocations. Exceptions may be made to this principle if the costs associated with tracking of actual usage outweigh the benefits. There are two main types of service chargebacks that are typically used. The first one is a *fixed based chargeback*, which is a fixed price or allocation amount that is agreed upon between support services and its customers. Here, price setting can become a very political process. Also, customers do not share any additional cost savings made by support services. The second option is *usage based chargeback*, in which the customers are charged based on the total cost or price allocated to perform the agreed upon services. Here, there is a lack of clarity between the performance offered to customers and the price they are charged.

- *Tracking costs*—IT will identify and track all costs associated with the delivery of IT services and will provide the IT clients insight into these costs where required. As illustrated below, the goal is to be able to allocate the costs to a specific service. A catalog is an overall listing or menu of what IT can offer the business through internal IT capabilities or relationships with external IT providers. The categories are logical groupings of items in the catalog to facilitate IT customer understanding or navigation of IT services. The services are individual items that IT customers "buy" and "consume" from IT, and IT services are packaged so that IT customers understand what they are buying and have business driver "levers" that enable them to control IT costs. IT offerings are a bundling of IT product and service components. The components are basic IT capabilities or technologies that are the building blocks of IT services. These have product components such as hardware, system software, networks, and applications, and also service components such as reporting, root cause analysis, and requirements definition.

Figure 18: Services Chargebacks

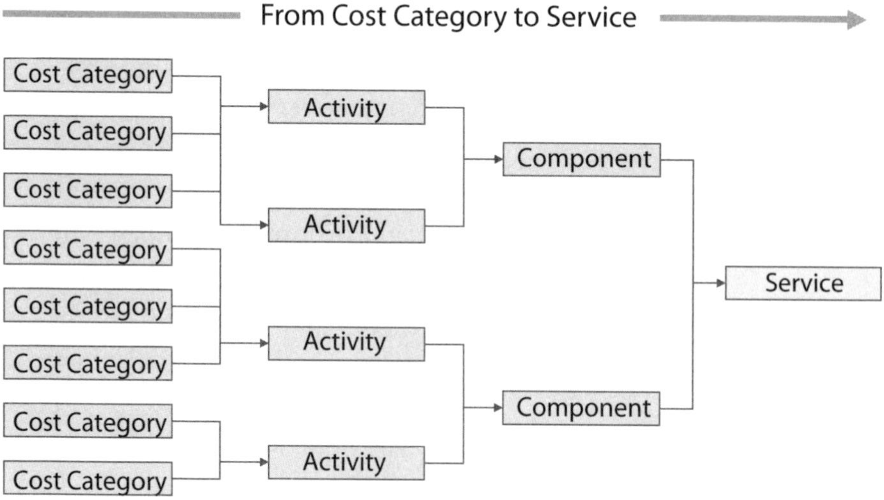

From Cost Category to Service

Some of the best practices in the industry for chargeback mechanisms are:

- Solicit input from operating unit clients—these are the people who will see shared services costs on their profit and loss statements.
- Ensure that chargeback data provided is easy to understand and is actionable.
- Establish stable pricing, where applicable, to support a joint planning process.
- Avoid creating a chargeback model that requires an "army" of accountants to administer.
- Avoid creating complicated allocation methodologies for immaterial balances.
- Utilize a chargeback method to encourage better business behavior throughout the organization.
- Operate as a business and establish a strong service provider/customer relationship.
- Conduct frequent comparative benchmarking studies; develop formal programs to move toward being best in class
- Separate legal entity/regulatory reporting from management reporting.

Enterprise Performance Management/Business Intelligence

The next best thing to knowing something is knowing where to find it.
—Author unknown

The origins of business intelligence can be found in the manner human cognition is used to make decisions. Whether we are faced with attending a conference, getting married, or investing in some back-office enterprise resource planning (ERP) system, we instinctively try to follow a process of observing, acting, evaluating, and recalibrating as needed.

When we are to make a decision, we first analyze the situation. We try to understand the characteristics of the circumstances and the environment. We then begin to evaluate our options. After some analysis we choose a certain course of action and act on it. Then we see the results, evaluate the results, and see how the situation is changed by internal actions and external influences. So information is the result of processing, manipulating, and organizing data in a way that adds knowledge to the receiver. Business intelligence capabilities are built exactly on the same process:

- *What is* happening?—Scorecards and dashboards
- *Why* did it happen?—Analytics
- What *will happen*?—Forecasting
- What *do we want to happen*?—Planning, budgeting, consolidation
- What *happened?*—Reporting

According to one story, Henry Ford was experiencing a difficulty at his factory and called in Thomas Edison to have a look. Edison took a look around, then marked an *X* in chalk on a wall of boilerplate, identifying the problem. Ford was ecstatic and told Edison to send him an invoice. The next day, a bill arrived for $10,000. When a flustered Ford asked for a breakdown of the charges, Edison sent another invoice, and this one listed a charge of $1 for the chalked *X* and $9,999 for knowing where to put it.

Figure 19: Business Intelligence Value Levers

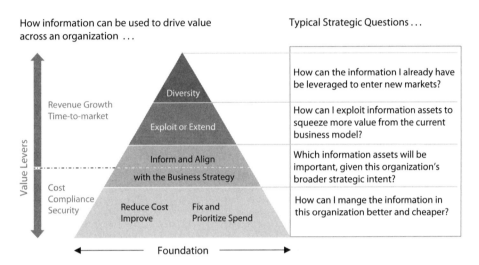

How information can be used to drive value across an organization . . .

Typical Strategic Questions . . .

Diversity	How can the information I already have be leveraged to enter new markets?
Exploit or Extend	How can I exploit information assets to squeeze more value from the current business model?
Inform and Align with the Business Strategy	Which information assets will be important, given this organization's broader strategic intent?
Reduce Cost Improve / Fix and Prioritize Spend	How can I mange the information in this organization better and cheaper?

Revenue Growth
Time-to-market

Cost
Compliance
Security

Value Levers

Foundation

But this area of IT has run into many problems because of an explosion of data and information. Storage costs have continued to fall and the structured and unstructured data being captured within an enterprise have been increasing exponentially. Companies are capturing and persisting transactional (structured) data, office/compound documents, faxes, images, photos, graphics, video and audio, web content, and other unstructured data feeds like emails, tweets, blog comments, etc. This surely has led to what industry gurus call "information entropy." The origin of the word "entropy" was in thermodynamics, where systems were described using *thermal energy* instead of temperature. Entropy was just a number by which the thermal energy in the system was multiplied. But eventually entropy was used as a term to measure the disorder in a

> Like anything else in our universe, left unmanaged all forms of information will decay and become less useful.

system. Like anything else in our universe, left unmanaged all forms of information will decay and become less useful because content loses its context and data loses its meaning (technologists call this metadata). The need for *information architecture* is established if one sees these signs of information entropy in the organization:

- The company has multiple analytics, portals, content management, and data integration applications.
- Metrics and benefits are difficult to define and baseline.
- The company is still measuring availability and reliability at the information silo level—data marts, databases, applications, etc.
- The company has not defined and implemented a comprehensive information management application model aligning information criticality, data retention, and speed of access with price/performance and usage of existing software solutions.
- The company displays reluctant ownership of data—data is often owned by IT instead of business units.

Information Supply Chain— Turning Data into Action

The way to look at what is needed for companies to use their data and harness it into usable information to make better decisions is depicted below. One has to look at the exhaustive stack of capabilities needed—infrastructure, applications sitting on that infrastructure, and processes sitting on top of these systems, along with the governance and architectural guidelines for the same.

Figure 20: Business Intelligence Technology Stack

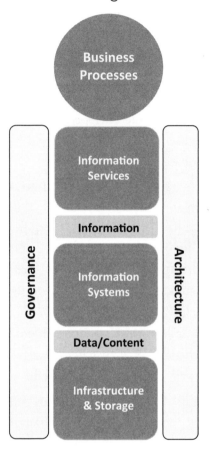

Business processes drive the activities that generate value and revenue for the enterprise. Supporting them with quality, timely information is critical. Business processes are a set of one or more linked activities that provide a specific service or product. The process can traverse many parts of an organization and even include external third parties. A clear understanding of the specific business processes is key to the enterprise, or specific areas of interest within the

> Business processes are a set of one or more linked activities that provide a specific service or product.

enterprise, in order to maximize value creation. Many businesses succeed without understanding their key business processes for some time. But eventually as the companies grow, businesses need to understand these interdependencies and focus on the key information, processes, and metrics that drive the most value. Whilst business architecture and business process diagrams can be used to map the complete enterprise, smaller, more pragmatic approaches can be used to identify and target high-value areas for further investigation.

Information services define, in business terms, the set of services required by the business to use and consume information. Each service describes the information required (e.g., customer profitability), the action(s) to be performed (online access, batch and ad-hoc reporting), the method of presentation (report, formatted data), and the attributes concerning the information (data quality, time lines, etc.).

Users want to use *information* independent from specific silo-ed applications. Information is usually an aggregate of a number of data sources and provides some useful knowledge which differentiates it from discrete data. This logical layer is usually defined in terms of information architecture, which describes the various information elements required by the business to function.

The *applications and systems* that manipulate and manage data provide the core functional capabilities of turning data into valued information. Information systems are the applications used to process information in the enterprise. Many of these systems will be interconnected, allowing the creation of information from across a number of different data sources that may (for example) individually serve separate business functions. These systems provide the key tools in order to manage and analyze information in the organization in the categories of analytics, enterprise search, content management, etc. Typically, a company's information system landscape has grown organically, being a mixture of (primary information) solutions designed to support specific business functions (e.g., marketing, finance) and (secondary) systems where information is stored in less structured formats (e.g., email, file stores, etc). IT/IS organizations are often trapped by competing demands to provide new capabilities to support the business and still reduce cost, improve quality, and increase compliance and performance.

Data and content provide the raw building blocks from which value—information—is derived. An understanding of the individual data elements, records, and documents, as well as their origin, location (system), and significance (in generating business insight and value) is important. Data and content are usually represented logically in a data structure or architecture diagram, which describe key attributes and mappings. The diagram can be used to support both the architectural and governance processes (e.g., master data management, records management), which have a direct impact on information provision and quality. Each of the data items can sit across a number of information systems, and in many organizations there will be duplication of data in various silos that will need to be addressed and possibly disputes around which of the data items is the master version.

The *physical infrastructure* drives performance, reliability, flexibility, and integration of the resulting services. The physical infrastructure is used to run the information systems and store the data within the enterprise. Key attributes of the physical infrastructure that are pertinent to the information domain include how infrastructure is administered, operated, and monitored. They also include the physical design and architecture of the computing assets, along with storage and transport capability. For many IT departments, their information systems are the source of many of their problems. For the large information systems, performance is poor and unpredictable, intersystem integration generates complex incidents, operational costs are high, and data volume growth is

> Unstructured data sources are unpredictable and generate a surprisingly high number of problems.

out of control. Unstructured data sources are unpredictable and generate a surprisingly high number of problems from users trying to find or access information from systems with traditionally lower service levels. An understanding of what information elements are important and the business's requirement to use that information can drive the right responses from IT to meet these needs. An information services catalog can provide the reference work for this insight.

End-to-end *data architecture* designs enable agility and alignment to business requirements. The information architecture capability provides a structured framework across all of the architectural disciplines. The goal of information and data architecture within the IT organization is to *store* (which systems store and own the data, how clean is it, and how is it stored on relational database systems), *organize* (data warehouses, data marts, taxonomy, master data management), *move* (data flows within and between applications, how data is extracted, transformed, and loaded), and *access* (knowing what you need to know, when you need it, and how to act upon it—reporting, analytics, etc.) data.

Information governance defines the rules, processes, and structures that will ensure that the information management vision is delivered and that day-to-day operations run smoothly. The governance structure will define clear accountabilities for ownership and decision making and will ensure that all standards and policies are met or approve exceptions where required. This governance will allow the execution of information lifecycle management, master data and metadata management, and information policy management. The governance structure will also approve changes to the strategy and road maps. Information governance is often patchy across a business. Where significant information-centric processes are supported by specific systems (e.g., data warehouses, ERP systems, etc.) there is often an individual or group that "owns" the use of the system and hence creates processes to support the management of the information/data. However, these approaches are rarely replicated across the enterprise. Where they do exist, they are often not consistent and do not cover all of the high-value business important information. Poor governance has a direct impact on data quality, cost, compliance, and security.

Data Rich, Information Poor?
Focus on the Right Metrics

I was once seated next to an executive on a flight and she was looking ever so zealously into her laptop screen at some kind of executive dashboard with nice looking charts. With my interest piqued, I grabbed the earliest opportunity to introduce myself and how business intelligence solutions were my bread and butter. She was delighted at my background and said that she was "looking at some KPIs from a recent e-marketing campaign, an email blast to some leads and customers." She talked about how overwhelmed she was with the different sets of numbers and how she sought a way to ferret out patterns that would help her business unit make better decisions. Later, recollecting our conversation, I realized that one hears so often about the importance of metrics, KPIs, measurement, and so on that it almost sounds clichéd to use the terminology.

Businesses cannot function without some kind of indicators of current performance and future forecasts of performances. I believe that the mantra of all enterprise performance management (EPM) efforts is what Six Sigma practitioners get their brains tattooed with:

- If you can't measure something, you really don't know much about it.
- If you don't know much about it, you can't control it.
- If you can't control it, you are at the mercy of chance.

This sums up the importance of measurement and how measured *data* translate into *information*, which finally morphs into *knowledge* or wisdom that can be used by the organization to create some sustainable competitive advantage. But before we explore why we need to measure and what we need to measure, it's good to understand the different nuances of measurement systems:

- A *measure* is a quantitative indication of the extent, amount, dimension, capacity, or size of some attribute of a product or a process. It is a single data point (e.g., number of defects from a single product review).

> *Data* translate into *information,* which finally morphs into *knowledge* or wisdom that can be used by the organization to create some sustainable competitive advantage.

- *Measurement* is the act of determining a measure.
- A *metric* is a measure of the degree to which a system or process possesses a certain attribute. Metrics relate data points to each other (e.g., average number of defects found in reviews). Metrics can be *directly* observable quantities (the number of source lines of code, number of man-hours, etc.) or can be *derived* from one or more directly observable quantities (defects per thousand lines of code, etc.).
- An *indicator* is a metric or series of metrics that provides insight into a process, project, or product. So indicators are metrics in a form suitable for assessing project behavior or process improvement. An indicator may be the behavior of a metric over time. Examples would include the number of trouble reports written and resolved over time, the number of requirements changes over time, etc. Indicators are used in conjunction with one another to provide a more complete picture of project behavior.

The challenge in doing business intelligence dashboards/metrics initiatives is that there is an assumption that the ultimate goal is to have a tool to enable leaders to continuously monitor and guide the business—the way a dashboard works for a pilot. But the reality is that successful leaders tend to want reports or met-

> The real goal is to focus executive questions on strategic issues as opposed to helping them "pilot" operations.

rics that help them validate and refine their own sense of the business—to see if their "gut feeling" is still right. The real goal is to focus executive questions on strategic issues as opposed to helping them "pilot" operations. And most thinking starts with questions around what metrics to use— "How much?", "How many?", etc. Before we begin thinking in those terms, it is good to analyze why metrics are really needed. The use of metrics or scorecards should encompass the following objectives:

- *Verify achievement* of deliverables associated with the initiative/project.
- *Behavior modifier*—Verify achievement of financial gains anticipated from the initiative/project.
- *Cause and effect relationships*—Verify benefits achieved were a result of the efforts of that particular initiative/project. People will find ways to get information they think they need, whether linked to their strategy or not. So thought needs to be given to establish the relationship between business outcomes and projects that are being undertaken.
- *Accountability* for results—Make sponsors accountable for results within their areas.
- Enable *reuse* of processes, models, etc. for future initiatives.

Whether one executes the enabling processes for decision making through balanced scorecards, dashboards, or reports, the focus is to be able to get the right information to the right people at the right time.

Figure 21: Right Information to the Right People at the Right Time

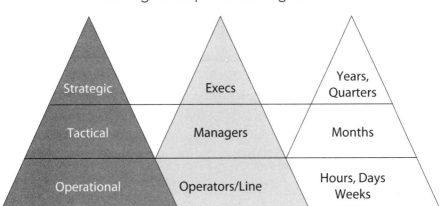

The typical process for getting the right metrics management in the company is as below:

- *Collect requirements*—Understand who the stakeholders are, what they would like to know, and why.
- *Define the metrics*—Define in detail what the metric will be, its purpose, how it is calculated, which source systems in the organizations will have the data, and who owns those systems from an IT management and business perspective. It is also important to capture the frequency of collection, trigger points, and potential methods of collection.
- *Establish metric target values*—Establish targets and performance ranges for each metric.
- *Collect metrics*—Create manual/automated workflows to be able to capture the data to calculate the metrics.
- *Report metrics*—Automate dashboard creation as much as possible and report the metrics at an agreed upon frequency to the right stakeholders.
- *Act upon metrics*—The metrics should provide the requisite feedback for the team and indicate that some further action/investigation/replanning is needed.

- *Refine metrics over time*—Any metric that has been established and is being produced on an ongoing basis should be revisited on a periodic basis. In some cases, once a metric is used and drives a positive change in the organization, then the metric has done its job and may no longer need to be generated (or may be generated less frequently than on a monthly basis). In other cases, new metrics will be added, and in some cases, targets could be reset for existing metrics.

The components of a successful metrics solution are as follows:

1. **Get the business leaders/customers involved (alignment)**—
   Get everyone marching to the same beat.
   Since the strategic vision of the company flows from the top down, the leaders need to be involved in how the metrics are linked to achieving their business goals. The executive leadership defines the *what, why,* and eventually *how* of the business, and the key success factor metrics will directly feed into the "*how*" of the business and should have answers to the following:
   - What should you measure?
   - How often should you measure?
   - Who is accountable for the metric?
   - What should you use as a benchmark?
   - Do the metrics reflect strategic business drivers? Do they correlate to competitive advantage?

As a general rule, the more closely numbers reflect what your customers value most, the better off those metrics will be.

Also, it is important to talk to the *customers*, because too many times performance metrics look inward, reflecting what operational managers think is important. As a general rule, the more closely numbers reflect what your customers value most, the better off those metrics will be.

2. **Limit the number of metrics**—*Avoid information overload.*
   In order to relay or derive valuable actions from the metrics, one should implement no more than a handful (seven or eight) of the metrics at a given time. Getting too bogged down in measurements, one will lose time and focus, employees will get confused, and upper managers may lose track of what you're doing. This blinding by numbers can actually prevent progress.

3. **Metrics must be defined**—*If it walks like a dog and barks like a dog, it's a dog.*
   A detailed description of the measurement process should be given in such a way that it can be easily understood. Generally called *operational definitions*, these include a precise definition of the characteristic and how, specifically, data collectors are to measure the characteristic.

4. **Automate the creation of metrics wherever possible**—
   Even a correct decision is wrong when it was taken too late.
   —Lee Iacocca, former CEO of Chrysler

   The automation of the metrics generation:
   - Enforces integrity of the source data.
   - Enforces integrity of the calculation.
   - Ensures time lines of the information.
   - Provides for repeatable, predictable results.

   There is always talk among IT and business users about structuring reports and measures to enable executives to drill down to root issues. While that is a good capability to have, the fact is that many metrics are difficult to drill down accurately. Also, most executives prefer to focus on directions and actions, and they expect others to analyze the root issues. So having a focus on the reality of what the business needs to make successful decisions and how the reports and measures have to be used is important.

5. **Visually represent the metrics**—*A picture is worth a thousand words.*

   Data, by itself, can be overwhelming and difficult to analyze. The human brain works best by building patterns of the data captured. Graphical representations of data can highlight important aspects within the data and assist the viewer in focusing on important items. In certain cases, visualization of information can assist the viewer in being more efficient with the analysis.

6. **Metrics should have a fast feedback loop**—*As someone said, Feedback is the shortest English word that contains* abcdef, *and it should be the breakfast of champions.*

   The measurement systems must provide feedback promptly so that you can identify problems and correct them as soon as possible. They should not be cumbersome or take a long time to yield data. Metrics should be kept simple; avoid setting up complex measurements that are difficult to use. The information they provide should be used to take direct action. Metrics should not complicate operations and create excessive overhead.

   There is always a tendency for metrics to get "stale," and they lose executive attention or interest after some time. Also, they are difficult to change and maintain as the business changes; they should enable some action taking.

7. **Ensure corrective action based on the metrics**—*It's not enough to aim, you must hit.*

   At the very outset, there should be thought given to the use of information gathered in addition to the metrics themselves. The process should ensure that the KPIs and metrics should provide the requisite feedback for the team to take corrective action as soon as possible.

8. **Create an auditing process for your metrics**—*If you don't ask the right questions, you won't get the right answers.*
   Since changing business conditions entail rethinking your business strategy often, it is important to protect the integrity of your metrics data.

9. **Don't overdo drill down structures and have role-based access**—*I have little patience with scientists who take a board of wood, look for its thinnest part, and drill a great number of holes where drilling is easy.*
   —Albert Einstein
   Don't overdo drill down structures. They are less flexible and harder to maintain, and many measures lose value at very low levels. Also, there is no such thing as "transparency" —reporting must respect rules about who can see what information in what sequence. Where all folks can see information or to which level they can drill down has to be driven by what their roles are— after the drill comes the screw.

10. **Perform sensitivity analyses on the metric**—*It is all a question of sensitiveness.*
    —D.H. Lawrence
    It is valuable to know the degree of importance of your business metrics. The data captured could have a linear or exponential influence on results. It may be that a scientific weighted average of different metrics is needed to remove certain management biases, such as in projects prioritization.

Using Six Sigma for Data Quality

Typically it's been seen that during the initial phases of a business intelligence (BI) or data warehouse (DW) effort there is generally a good focus on data architecture and the right components to build the operational data store (ODS), enterprise data warehouse (EDW), and reporting architecture. But somehow the importance or focus on data quality is typically lukewarm at best. There is always a good understanding of its significance initially, but as progress is made in requirements and design, the overwhelming list of activities around modeling, data capture, and extract, transform, load (ETL) routines makes the team lose focus on data quality. And eventually comments like these pop up: "Our data *isn't synchronized*. Daily transaction files didn't match with the customer data." "Data was extracted by an individual user, then passed around to other users who don't understand the context of the data or its *relationship to other applications*." "Oh, but we have multiple sources for the same data." "Important entities and their attributes are hidden and floating in text fields."

And usually in situations like these, folks with data quality experience are brought in to clean up the data problems and still try to achieve the business benefits that were originally built in to the business case. If the system involves data integration from a number of disparate sources (which it usually does), it is useful at times to follow a *bifocal data quality strategy* (short term and long term) to ensure that the projects achieve their business objectives. In the short term, we can look at tactical ways to improve data quality using data profiling, data cleansing, and enhancement. The long-term strategy should be to implement an ongoing data quality initiative that provides a cost-effective operational data architecture for the management, storage, transformation, and delivery of data. This section details the high-level approach for both strategies and organizations, so they can pick their place on the spectrum depending upon their appetite for investment and their focus on data quality.

Before deciding what level of investment to make in data quality efforts, it is worthwhile to consider the following key questions about the BI/DW initiative being undertaken by the organization:

- How much quality of data is needed? The context of data quality should be the level of data quality needed for a business functionality; otherwise, theoretically, one can spend infinite cycles to get the right quality.

- Do business and IT users view quality data as a prerequisite? Is the quality of data considered in system and business planning? Is the quality of the data investigated *prior to* system design?

- Are subject areas prioritized based on their importance to the business strategy?

- Has a data quality program with dedicated employees been set up?

- Does the data governance organization identify business sponsors to provide ownership, accountability, direction, and buy-in for data quality improvements? Good data ownership is essential to proper data lineage and execution of data quality effort.

- Are quantifiable metrics for a data quality baseline available and monitored on a regular basis?

- Does the team use data definition dictionaries to define fields and their meanings? Are changes to fields and data managed through a change request mechanism in place to measure and report the impact of changes to field definitions?

- Are cross-field validations defined by the business and systematically enforced at the point of entry?

- Is there an archive and purging strategy to retire data that has exceeded its valuable lifespan?

Depending on your initial assessment, if the general direction is to work toward some quick wins, then you need to follow a short-term data quality effort to clean up the existing data sources. I have found the following brief structure (DMAIC) borrowed from Six Sigma methodology is very useful and practical. I have used this in one- to two-week cycles dealing with different source systems and following a rhythm beat to tackle some tactical data quality issues. These steps have been briefly addressed previously, but are discussed in more detail below:

Define

Definition is the first step, and it is key. As Albert Einstein once said, "If I had an hour to save the world, I would spend fifty-nine minutes defining the problem and one minute finding solutions."

Even if an elaborate effort has *not* been made to execute a central metadata repository, the initial task for the data management team should be to identify all production files from source systems and define the important fields and expected values. This information can be received from metadata repositories, enterprise repositories, and data dictionaries. The IT organization can also extract data from data definition artifacts like COBOL copybooks, PL/1 data, and database catalogs. The results of these findings could be stored in a repository like MS Excel. An example of the ideal set of data architecture artifacts is below. The data dictionary is a key document used through all phases of an implementation, and this helps create a data dictionary.

Measure

Now the data architecture team should start profiling this data using tools like Informatica profiler or just simple PL/SQL queries. They should create data reports to define a data quality baseline. The team should inspect data values—value/frequency list, boundary points (high/low values), and values with special characters.

This activity can help take counts of values that are nulls or missing values, unique values, and constant values or code values. The team should look for usage of columns—low usage columns (a high percentage of blanks or zeros), unused data values from code tables, and indications of a "no value" like null, blank, "n/a", etc. The team should also inspect structure and look for orphaned records or referential integrity. There are tools that help in pattern recognition (i.e., check for predefined formats and the frequency of each pattern), such as with telephone numbers—with and without dashes and parentheses; social security numbers—with and without dashes; zip codes—with and without the PLUS 4 field; etc.

At this stage the team should also look for derived values and computations like PROFIT = REVENUE – COST or business rules like "If CUSTOMER_TYPE = 'PREFRRED' then DISCOUNT = 10%." The deliverable output could be in the form of a report composed of a list of defects annotated with key information, such as impact on the business, criticality level, frequency, and possible resolutions. For example:

System	Object	Field	Description	Count	Impact	Correction Effort	Action

1. **System**—Name of the system in which the error/defect was found
2. **Object**—Name of the object (entity, table) where the error/defect was found
3. **Field**—Name of the field (attribute, label) related to the error
4. **Description of error**—Detailed description of the defect
5. **Count**—Number of errors that were found of this error type
6. **Impact**—Depending on the understanding of the impact on business functionality and its importance, categorize the defect as critical, high, medium, or low

7. **Correction effort**—This is to explain the time and effort it might take to correct an error of this category
8. **Action**—This is to explain how this error type could be handled; for example, create automated update scripts, manually cleanse in-source system, no action, etc.

Analyze

Once all of this data has been captured and measured, the team needs to start grouping specific data issues into more generic observations. They need to identify the root cause by asking business subject matter experts (SMEs), developers, and technical experts. They can then formulate recommendations on how to tackle specific issues.

Observation	Impact	Root cause	Recommendation

Improve

The data quality team then needs to work with development teams and source system teams to have the teams update. They need to update their data dictionary with values expected for code value fields as well as data attribute definitions with any new discoveries about the data. They need to facilitate consensus on new transformations required and/or unique aspects of data attributes.

Control

There should be ongoing monitoring of the critical data quality metrics to ensure that the cleaned data does not fall below a quality threshold. People often believe that once a fix has been identified and applied, a given problem will remain resolved forever. While this is often the case, things are rarely that simple when people and processes are involved. Ongoing measurement against the stored quality data is advisable.

After your team has helped alleviate some immediate and tactical data problems, you can start laying the foundation for a *long-term data quality strategy* with the following guidelines:

> People often believe that once a fix has been identified and applied, a given problem will remain resolved forever.

1. Data quality initiatives need to encompass improvements in all aspects of the enterprise: people, processes, and technology.

   - *People:* Establish data governance organization(s) to provide ownership, accountability, direction, and buy-in for data quality improvements. It addresses the processes, skills, leadership, and assets required to successfully administer a company's information resources. This involves data administration, a data quality services team, a data governance committee, DBAs, some business and executive members, etc.

   - *Processes:* Streamline data setup and maintenance processes to minimize handoffs. This, in turn, will reduce the risk of introducing errors into the system. Since you have just cleaned up the major data quality issues, strict data governance needs to be enforced from this point forward. This involves a *formal* change request process for any changes to metadata or data artifacts; proper approvals for any changes (from the team, delivery manager, data champion, and anyone who could be impacted by the change); and proper recording of any changes (how many changes were done, how many are approved but pending implementation, how many are pending approval, and how many were rejected and why). This should be stored in a tool that has the audit trail available to the team. Timestamps are necessary for when the change was requested, when it was implemented, and by whom.

- *Tools:* Implement system controls to reduce the introduction of errors at the point of entry. Implement data profiling/data quality toolsets to help assess and monitor the health of the data. This involves data profiling, quality and monitoring tools, ETL tools, and audit reports.

2. Key subject areas for data quality improvements should be *prioritized* relative to their importance to key business strategies and initiatives. Also, enough time should be allocated for subject matter experts to support the data quality team in profiling the source systems and analyzing data quality concerns. The data samples provided should be over a significant period of time (at least a quarter if possible and preferably a whole year). When data is originating from the mainframe, this data should be staged so anomalies can be scrutinized with more care using SQL statements. This also makes it easier to set up tools like Informatica Profiler, Power Analyzer, etc., which are used to profile the data.

> Data Profiling should be performed during the analysis phase of the project to ensure the business needs are going to be met by the source.

3. There should be a proper process for defining what level of data quality is needed for the compensation systems and any outbound interfaces. The business analysts should be asked and a formal DQ definition document should contain things like threshold levels for nulls, spaces, negative values, etc. This should be formally signed off on.

4. A data quality assessment plan should be created. This plan should be used to validate the data definitions and rules. *Data profiling* should be performed during the analysis phase of the project to ensure the business needs are going to be met by

the source. Without a minimum level of data quality, the data source should not be used and alternative sources should be sought. The following is a data profiling template that could be used for all data elements.

Category	Field	Description
Description		
	Data element name	Commonly agreed, unique data element name from the application domain.
	Description	Description/Definition of the element in the application domain.
	Data format	Data type (characters, numeric, etc.), size, and, if needed, special representation.
	Default value	Data element may have a default value.
	Example	Provide an example of the data.
	Reference	Provide reference to other data elements, applications, or documents.
Data Quality Controls		
	Range list	Range of acceptable values for the data element, if applicable.
	Inter-element validation details or reference to other documents	Validation rules between this element and other elements in the data dictionary.

Related Metadata		
	Data owner	The Business Owner of the data element.
	External references	References to books, other documents, laws, etc.
Data Profile Test	**Date of Test**	**Issue—result**
Domain checking (allowable values)		
Range checking		
Name standardization		
Referential integrity		
Basic stats, frequencies, ranges		
Duplicate identification		
Uniqueness and missing value validation		
Key identification		
Data rule compliance		

5. During the analysis and design phases, the data needs to be defined in both technical and business terms. Examples of technical terms are data type, length, or number of decimal places. This definition step also captures any rules the data should satisfy.

6. These definitions should be included in the data map and data dictionary. The data maps should have data type definitions, ranges, lengths, and description of columns.

7. The data map should be the one true source of data definition for the project. The data in the data map should also be in sync with data as defined in the corporate metadata repository. The data map should include data information for all operational data stores, data warehouses, data marts, views, etc.

8. The data architecture team should be hands on during the analysis and design phase with artifacts like logical data model, physical data model, data maps, etc. This team should also be involved in reviews for the ETL development process during implementation and should partake in code reviews, etc.

9. After the data artifacts are finalized, any data object change should go through a data change request process involving a committee represented by team members from data architecture, development, business analysis, and testing.

10. Like any other corporate effort, proper communication is key to the success of the data quality initiative. Raising awareness of the project and frequently communicating the benefits of the efforts will help the adoption of a culture where data is viewed as a corporate asset.

Analytics—Competitive Intelligence

Wise men say, and not without reason, that whoever
wished to foresee the future might consult the past.
—Machiavelli, Italian statesman and philosopher

It ain't what we know that hurts us.
It's what we know that just ain't so.
—Will Rogers, American humorist, social commentator, and actor

Analytics is the use of data, statistical and quantitative analyses, explanatory and predictive models, and fact-based management to drive decisions and actions. With the advance in information management systems, companies are able to run scenarios in their systems to understand what's going on in operations, financials, marketing, etc. As someone said, "There are phases of human emotions, so dictated by business intelligence systems. *Analytical curiosity* quickly changes to *analytical despair*, then *analytical rage*—and then IT management organization gets the call to clean up the systems and software mess."

The way to see how business intelligence is evolving more into competitive intelligence is how this technology and its processes are helping analyze information, as shown in the figure below:

- *Stage 1 – Reporting—What* happened?
- *Stage 2 – Analyzing—Why* did it happen?
- *Stage 3 – Predicting—What will* happen?
- *Stage 4 – Operationalizing—What is* happening (real-time)?
- *Stage 5 – Active warehousing*—What do we *want* to happen?

There are many different approaches to building these analytic systems within an organization depending upon what the goals of a business or its units are.

- *Monte Carlo simulation*—This technique uses data to establish a pattern between a domain of possible inputs. The calculations generate inputs randomly from a probability distribution over the domain, perform computations on these, and aggregate the results. This tries to minimize reinventing the wheel by reuse of research results. In the pharmaceutical industry, for example, during the discovery phase of their value chain, data mining is used to search contextual information based on secondary relationships.

- *Yield management*—A market segmentation strategy to capture the consumer surplus, widely used in the entertainment and hospitality industries. Airlines, hotels, theme parks, car rentals, cruise ships, broadcasting (TV, radio), and utilities (telecom, electricity), for example, always used segmentation and peak-load pricing. But with the advent of the computing power of systems this technique is now able to do excessive and data-intensive calculations with linear programming to optimize revenue. This utilizes scientific models to predict demand and availability; optimize pricing and yield through integration of predictive forecasts, guest value, and local market conditions; and push automated rates and offers through optimal channels. Just like airlines realized long ago that a plane flying with an empty seat is forgone revenue, many companies use historical data to optimize differential revenue gains. American Airlines added $1.4 billion additional revenue over a three-year period in the early 1990s. Hertz added 1 to 5 percent revenue annually, and so did companies like Marriott Hotels and Royal Caribbean Cruise Line. Computer algorithms can use variables like time of purchase/usage (advance/spot purchase, day-of-week/season), purchase restrictions (cancellation options, minimum term, Saturday night stay), purchase volume (individual vs. group), and duration of usage (single night/weekly rate) to get the right price to the right customer. The next time you are stuck at an airport and an airline has mentioned an over-booked flight, know that some computer algorithm was doing some marginal analysis based on the capacity of the flight, typical cancellation rate, revenue from booking seats, and cost of denied boarding (these days, airlines under pressure are also adding costs like loss of goodwill along with the free flights they give you).

- *Regression analysis*—This is a set of techniques used for modeling and analyzing several variables and establishing a relationship between a dependent variable and one or more independent variables. It is widely used in marketing and sales as part of a company's value chain since it can provide deep insight into customer behavior and provide enhanced decision making for future customer interactions. Companies are using industrialized analytics, which uses closed-loop promotion and data mining to optimize marketing budget allocation (i.e., optimize marketing channel and product mix). The closed-loop promotion ensures feedback of mission-critical data to marketing and provides on-demand access to marketing decision-support. This helps create an optimal marketing mix (Jerome McCarthy called this the four P's—product, price, place, and promotion).

  The practice of analytics started with improvements in systems for statistical analysis that helped show why certain things were happening in the business environment. These were heavily used to do web traffic analyses during the emergence of e-commerce. Then these systems were extended to forecasting and extrapolation to see what would happen if the trends continued. Then the era of predictive modeling built systems that could try to predict what would happen next, based on empirical data and heuristics. Of course, all these systems are used to help with optimization of spend and maximization of revenue. As an example, within the financial services industry, specifically banks, such models are used to predict retention and loyalty, perform portfolio analytics, and help with fraud (transaction/payment) and anti–money laundering efforts.

They help answer questions in areas like *bank servicing*—Which customers/segments are at risk? Which ones are profitable? How do I retain them? How do I win back customers? They can also help with *loyalty programs*—What drives loyalty for my customer base? How do I design an effective loyalty program? They are used for *cross selling and upselling*—Which deposit account holders would be interested in an auto loan? Can we sell insurance along with auto loans? Which products can be sold on a credit card welcome call? Which "Gold" customers would increase their spend if we upgrade them to "Platinum"? Can I identify customers requiring short-term loans? It helps with *campaign management* with segmentation modeling, profitability analysis, retention campaigns, win-back campaigns, etc.

- *Neural Network Analysis*: Apart from the obvious impact in the study of real biological neurons, this technique is used in areas like distribution and logistics, sociology, and economics. Any company that produces a product is chartered with getting that product to its customers (whether that's the final customer, retailer, wholesaler, etc.) in the least expensive manner. They are constantly trying to reduce total inventory while maintaining service levels of supply at each warehouse or distribution center location. Neural network models help to optimize the variables involved: number of warehouses to have, location of each warehouse, size of each warehouse, allocation of products to the different warehouses, allocation of customers to each warehouse, etc. The objective is to balance service level of supply against production or purchasing costs, inventory carrying costs, facility costs (storage, handling, and fixed costs), and transportation costs.

These analytics capabilities help organizations answer the key business questions:

- How do I get insight into the right consumer needs and opportunities for us to go after? This set of information can help support marketing decisions by making a factually up-to-date and complete picture of the customer information available from various internal and external sources. This can also establish a set of definitions and standards for commercial data and reporting.

- Where should I place my bets on a global stage across so many countries, categories, and brands? Analytics solutions can help companies better understand where to invest in sales and marketing and also help understand the bottom line of individual marketing initiatives and brand/channel/customer combinations. Many analytic systems are able to simulate the effects of important decisions and events.

- How can I make sure each part of my organization gets from point A to point B as in our strategic plan? Analytic solutions can help reduce ongoing loss of marketing know-how even with the rotation of marketers across different marketing media.

The majority of enterprises and service providers today focus on extracting relevant data and applying methods and algorithms to derive insights. There is greater value in looking at the entire value chain of analytics and extending the scope beyond methods and algorithms to include driving to outcomes. Therefore, true value from analytics requires a combination of key and relevant data, methods and algorithms to derive insights from the data, and processes to react to the insights and impact outcomes.

As companies mature, their requirements for business intelligence become more sophisticated. As one example, Google Inc. started out in 1998 with two guys working in a garage. A year later, they still only had eight employees, but by June of 2000 they were the world's largest search engine. They now employ over twenty thousand people, with offices around the world and a wide array of products and initiatives, and their homepage is one of the most visited sites on the Internet. According to their posted corporate history, in 2009 alone they generated a total of $54 billion of economic activity for American businesses, website publishers, and nonprofits. Their business intelligence requirements today are vastly different from their early garage days.

> Decision support capability may be deployed throughout an organization or even out to customers and partners.

Decision support capability may be deployed throughout an organization or even out to customers and partners. The key strategic questions around such capabilities are:

- How fast will the market grow, and at what pace will the nature of demand get more sophisticated (i.e., historic to predictive, functional to multi-functional)?
- Historic to predictive: Should we develop a specialty practice around quantitative analytics and hire expert statistical and domain skills?
- Functional to multi-functional: How do we integrate some

of the key functional offerings to make a more powerful integrated offering, and what kinds of skills do we need to cultivate at scale?

- How do our current offerings map to this matrix, where do we need to move, and at what pace?

Figure 22: Evolution of Analytics

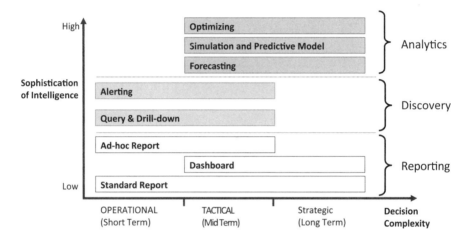

Customer Relationship Management

Customer service is not a department, it's an attitude.
—Unknown

Although your customers won't love you if you
give bad service, your competitors will.
—Kate Zabriskie, learning industry veteran, Business Training Works, Inc.

CRM is about using technology to enable marketers to do basic marketing better and achieve many of the benefits that were given up in mass marketing. The main premise of all CRM systems is that the consumer of a product or service is firstly driven by the need for information—I *want to know*. After that phase, he or she wants to conduct the transaction—I *want to have*. This then evolves into the need for a relationship—I *want to interact*—and then comes the final immersion—I *want to be engaged*. This is driven by knowing what the customer experience should be and by understanding why and how people interact with businesses.

> I want to know.
> I want to have.
> I want to interact.
> I want to be engaged.

As Mohanbir Sawhney said in *Business 2.0* (November 2003),

The limitations of space have long dictated the economics of exchange transactions . . . In the Network Economy, the limitations of space no longer apply . . . But a funny thing happened on the path to frictionless capitalism. The economics of distance died, but the economics of attention took its place . . . But in many markets, customers find themselves overwhelmed with vendors clamoring for their attention, and vendors find themselves in a desperate battle to acquire customers. Customers still need to search, evaluate, negotiate, and configure products on their own. What customers gained in reduced transportation costs, they seem to have lost in increased search costs. These search and evaluation costs continue to create significant friction in commerce.

An example of a digital customer is as below, where the customer is activity focused, not product focused:

Figure 23: Customer Experience

Mark Klein and Arthur Einstein wrote in the magazine *strategy+business* (October 2003), "Why are customers who say they're satisfied not necessarily repeat customers? Because satisfaction is a measure of what people say, whereas loyalty is a measure of what they actually do. Many managers still don't recognize this fundamental difference, so they use customer satisfaction and customer loyalty interchangeably, as though they were synonyms."

To orchestrate positive experiences, businesses must have a thorough understanding of their customers' activities, behaviors, options, and concerns.

To orchestrate positive experiences, businesses must have a thorough understanding of their customers' activities, behaviors, options, and concerns. Customer experience factors like convenience, customization, choice, context, control, and being part of a community are important. And some other trends that are becoming more and more prominent in this global economy are as follows:

- Customers are becoming more diverse, discriminating, and empowered.
- Demographic and social changes are creating a more diverse, fragmented consumer base and buyer values.
- Exponential expansion of media options makes targeting consumers far more complex.
- Products/services, stores, and messages are proliferating and becoming increasingly commoditized.
- "Cash-rich, time-poor" consumers are demanding more relevant offerings, experiences, and communication.
- Consumers are far more technology savvy and more active in controlling the consumption cycle.

This has led to a need for mastering customer-centric execution, which increases an organization's pace, certainty, and strategic flexibility. Every company understands that it needs to become "customer relevant" and has to deliver a differentiated customer experience through marketing, sales and service synchronization, adaptive supply chains, and retailization of products and services. In almost every industry there is a global shift to engaging the customer as part of the workforce, by letting them choose the kinds of service and products they want. So the customer-engaged innovation of incorporating the customer into the experience of creating and consuming products and service has put a new emphasis on newer CRM systems. In such an ecosystem, businesses will need to consider many aspects of customer lifetime value: acquisition cost, retention cost, base profits from transactions, revenue growth, referrals, and price premium as depicted in the following figure.

What this shows is that as the company matures from "acquiring" customers to "developing" them and then "retaining" them, the value to their top line and bottom line increases accordingly.

Figure 24: Value Creation through CRM

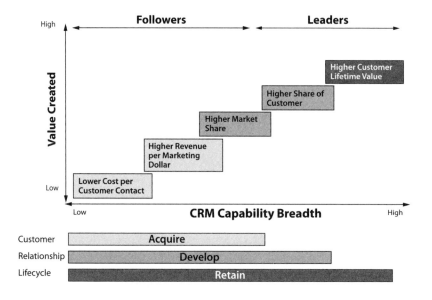

A good framework for such capabilities has three main components: insight-driven marketing (which comes out of marketing ROI, brand, customers, products, and channels), customer segmentation and targeting (made possible through customer insight, data mining, segmentation, and prognosis), and customer contact transformation (made possible by customer interaction and integrated contact-management).

Insight-Driven Marketing

The importance of good insight-driven marketing has existed since companies started on this planet. Everyone knows that to inform and convince the customer to consume products or services, one needs to understand one's customers. The revenue potential is that it leads to improved upselling and closing rates and the cost potential is that it leads to effective marketing spend and lower attrition costs of customers. Mature CRM systems should provide an integrated approach to marketing, sales, and customer service. They enable enterprises to raise sales effectiveness, efficiency of interactions, and customer satisfaction with customers across all channels—phone, web, sales force, email, fax, etc.

To deliver value, CRM has to integrate marketing and sales processes to be completed with the following functions: opportunity identification, deal management, research distribution, and automation of marketing functions (e.g., events organization). Customer data remains necessary for accurately gauging customer needs and predicting interactions. Esther Dyson summed it up in the magazine *strategy+business* (December 2009):

> People spend a lot of time online not looking for something, or at least not for something that can be bought or sold. Marketers need to understand that the Web is not about them; it's about us. Marketers and media sites keep thinking, "Well, if we can only tweak our banner ads right, we can get the same success rate as Google." But they can't, because a banner ad is usually shown to someone who is not looking for the item advertised.

The biggest component of establishing a robust platform for insight-driven marketing is to gather good and relevant customer data. The key is to manage what data about which customers is gathered in what manner from which sources—existing technology at touch points (point of sales, etc.) and the back office are often good internal sources. Companies do this collection of customer

> The biggest component of establishing a robust platform for insight-driven marketing is to gather good and relevant customer data.

information from various internal sources, including customer transactional information and other customer interaction information (e.g., customer contact history). Also, with the advent of market data aggregators, the acquisition of data from external sources is very prevalent to enhance the customer/prospect database. Data collection and the approach to defining customer data requirements, data integration across channels, data ownership, and data quality assurance are all important in building a healthy analytical system. Companies have to pay attention to the legal implications, privacy requirements, and so forth when collecting this data. As one example, in February the California Supreme Court reversed an earlier Court of Appeal ruling and ruled that the collection of zip codes by retailers—with some exceptions, such as proving identification—violates the California Civil Code and makes retailers subject to financial penalties, even retroactively from the ruling.

Some of the indicators of maturity in customer data acquisition are that the customer data is integrated across most integration channels and that executive management and business units actively support customer relationship focus and strategies. Customer information to be collected is proactively defined across all strategic business capabilities, and all customer contact interactions and transactions are collected and integrated. All channel data, including business partner information, is captured, and most of the data refreshes or updates occur dynamically.

Once this customer data is collected, the management of this information is key as well. Data architectures should be established for the delivery of customer data through interaction channels and for information sharing. This also supports customer data mining, ad-hoc queries, and marketing campaign execution. Some of the indicators of maturity in customer data management are that consistent customer IDs are used at all points of data capture and data repositories and there are minimal data redundancy issues. All contact channels share a common interaction database, and most data refreshes or updates occur dynamically.

Customer insight is gained through online sources, back office subscribers, external searches, and customer contacts made in sales centers. Once the insights are obtained, data management processes need to extract, cleanse, de-duplicate and match data, and load the information to the data warehouse. The data warehouse makes unique customer identification possible by providing information on bookings, subscriptions and registrations, profiles, searches, contact history, and campaign history. Thus customer insight and segmentation provide for business intelligence, reporting, segmentation, marketing analytics, and list management.

Figure 25: Customer Insight Through
Adequate Data Systems

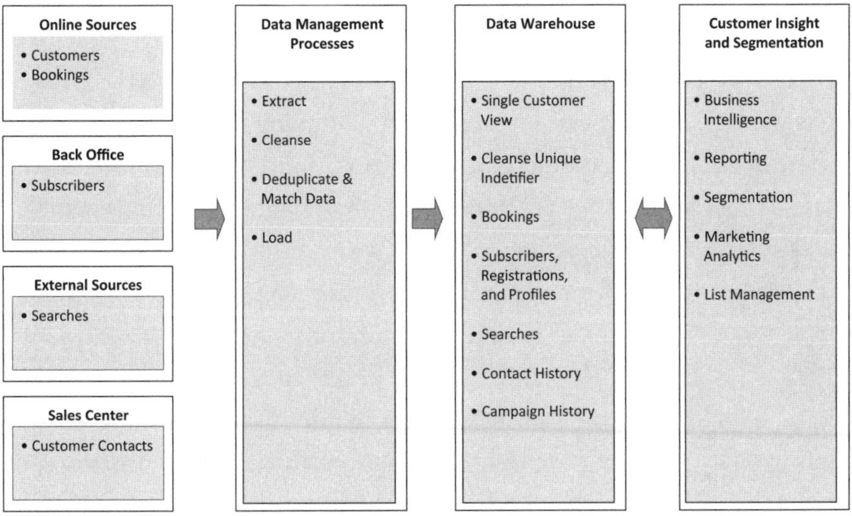

Customer Segmentation and Targeting

The key to creating customer segmentation and to targeting the right customers is to have adequate insight and to drive interactions with customers as per that insight. IT offers systems that can model and score customer and prospect bases by critical attributes (e.g., needs, behaviors, value). These systems have the ability to perform data exploration, querying, and reporting on customers and to offer database-driven data analyses that group customers into logical segments with similar characteristics and identify segment attributes and profiles. This insight is utilized to design the customer proposition(s), campaigns, and even product development. This helps in the development of marketing strategies, including prioritization between customer acquisition, development, retention, and cost-to-serve. The processes and system capabilities employed in developing marketing campaigns for specific offers can help with efficient and effective execution of these campaign programs. The revenue potential is drastically improved cross selling.

Customer Touch Point Transformation

These days customers interact with companies at many touch points—call centers, online, mobile apps, point of sales in the case of the retail industry, etc. In order to offer a complete and holistic experience for the customer, the company should look at contact touch point transformation at every level. The revenue potential is improved longtime customer retention, and the cost potential is reduced attrition costs. The companies have to manage customer interaction by aligning processes, products, and offers with the appropriate channels. Many technologies like instant voice recognition (IVR) or computer telephony integration (CTI) provide the ability to access real-time and historical information regarding the quality of customer

> In order to offer a complete and holistic experience for the customer, the company should look at contact touch point transformation at every level.

interactions, which is key. These days speech recognition is also being used to improve customer interaction. Speech recognition is the use of computers to hear and understand spoken words. A speech recognition application allows the user to answer questions and provide information using a normal speaking voice. The most promising use of the technology in business is to allow users (customers) to interact with a computer over the telephone. A common application of this is the voice portal.

As computers tend to become more ubiquitous and less visible, the keyboard and mouse will eventually lose out to speech recognition technology as the primary way to communicate with computers. And so many other human machine interface (HMI) technologies like text-to-voice, voice-to-text, digital pens, and handwriting recognition enable companies to apply processes that provide a consistent approach to handling customer interactions. Creating a culture that is customer centric, attracting the right people, and training them to support this culture are key steps.

The Impact of Social Media on CRM

Ever since Morton Deutsch created the "social interdependence theory" in which he organized relationships into socially independent and interdependent categories, the bottom line is that individuals who share common goals will be affected by the actions of each other and their cooperation for information and action will lead to higher achievement. Nowhere is this seen so prevalently as in the emergence of social media technologies. This is highlighted by the story of Wikipedia, which demonstrates that the sum total of a community can create phenomenal results. Wikipedia has its origins in Nupedia, which was created in 2000 and was to feature expert-written, peer-reviewed content. But the slow contribution of content posed a major problem. To spur faster production of content, Jimmy Wales and Larry Sanger created Wikipedia, to which anyone could contribute without editorial review. Wikipedia.com went live on January 15, 2001, and the new model expanded very quickly. Even with the risk of vandalism (such as contradictory or defamatory content) and concerns about accuracy of the data, this grew to be a great social experiment because people actually corrected defects and prevented content from overall vandalism.

Some people wonder if social media, social networking, and social CRM are just a fad. They wonder if maybe the folks weaving together these skeins of communities are really changing the world. But the impact and reach is evident by the speed with which this area of consumer engagement is affecting us. Consider the time it took for the following media types to achieve fifty million users:

- Radio = 38 years
- TV = 13 years
- Web = 4 years
- Facebook = 3.5 years

And then one wonders how these tools are changing the way people work, live, and interact. People's lives have been changing since the mobile media arrived. When at work, so many of us check our personal emails. And when at home the work never stops. With emails popping on smart phones, everyone expects some response right away, especially if the matters are important. The line between personal and work lives is fusing. And with the social media and network onslaught, schedules are going from fixed to continuous, interactions from one-to-one to one-to-many, and engagement is becoming more collaborative. The key is to also understand the demarcation of the channels within social media, so I wanted to document those as follows.

> With the social media and network onslaught, schedules are going from fixed to continuous, interactions from one-to-one to one-to-many, and engagement is becoming more collaborative.

Blogs: A website displays one person or organization's opinions on a topic and then allows comments. Similar to an online newspaper column, except unedited. One example is WordPress (My blog is also WordPress based—www.AshuBahtia.com.)

Open micro-blog: A site on which people post short comments that are then broadcast to all other users (e.g., Twitter). Private messages and direct messages are possible.

Closed micro-blog: Closed micro-blogs are sites that allow a micro-blogging service but protect it from being visible to everybody through firewalls and access criteria. Generally, they are used to communicate within a company, quickly and efficiently (e.g., Yammer).

Open social network: Open social networks are sites where users post information about themselves online and create connections between themselves and "friends." Access to users' information is unrestricted. Convention encourages the forging of new connections. Open social networks are akin to giving each user his or her own web page to do with as desired (e.g., MySpace).

Closed social network: Closed social networks are sites that allow networking via an invitation system. Only after an invitation to share information has been accepted can the parties access each other's details and updates (e.g., Facebook).

Due to all these channels, the way to do business may not have changed completely, but it has been influenced immeasurably. In the earlier days, companies talked and "told" people what to do, and 95 percent happy customers were good for

> Due to all these channels, the way to do business may not have changed completely, but it has been influenced immeasurably.

the company's bottom line. In these days, especially for B2C companies, the consumers are talking among themselves, so for companies it's time to "listen," and they have to go where the consumers hang out. And the 5 percent of unhappy customers can be bad for your business because their discontent spreads pretty fast and competitors can rapidly fill the gap. But these social channels also offer an opportunity, since they can increase brand engagement, trust, and loyalty. A McKinsey global survey in 2010 found that these tools/channels can seriously help increase marketing effectiveness and reduce some marketing costs.

By having a Twitter page, Comcast gets a face for the customer. Instead of waiting on the phone on hold, customers can tweet to Comcast Cares. Comcast can instantly build a brand by actively listening to customers' complaints and reaching out to them.

The other aspect of social media is how we use it for our cognitive learning. Howard Gardner described in his theory of multiple intelligences that we all have different dimensions of intelligence—interpersonal, intrapersonal, spatial, linguistic, logical–mathematical, existential, etc. Social media seems to have touched all of them and is taking deeper roots in each.

Talking to so many leaders in this area, I have realized that leaders must take the first critical step of changing their mindsets and revising some long-held beliefs about building and managing customer relationships and creating the right networks. In January 2009, the *Washington Post* ran an article about a top Indian retail company, one employing forty thousand people and operating one thousand stores, that hired a "chief belief officer" to boost their brand building with what he calls the "3-B model": belief, behavior, and business. This business strategist, speaking of modern corporate management, explained: "Business is run on a pattern of behavior. I help create the belief that governs that behavior." After examining the connections between belief, behavior, and business, the company reported that it experienced less attrition and better connections with customers. Sometimes even long-held beliefs must be changed, so that behavior will follow and the business will profit.

As Patricia Seybold wrote in *Business 2.0*, "Economists have been writing about the Network Effect since 1974, intrigued by the notion that, once a network is established, scarcity isn't the source of perceived value; instead, ubiquity is. In the physical world, the more fishers who come to a lake, the fewer fish each one will catch; the lower the benefit, and hence the value, for each one. In the cyber-world, on the other hand, the more people who participate in an online network, the greater the benefit—the larger the network, the greater the likelihood that you'll find the person, information, or resource you're seeking. The difference between these two analogies is simple. Fishers aren't adding fish to the lake; online users are."

The traditional principles were focused on the four *P*s of marketing—product, promotion, price, and place. But the fifth *P*—*people*—and their engagement for brand creation, for consistent and appealing experience, and for adding value to them through interactions is key. Social CRM is not only about a new channel but also about a fundamental shift in how to engage and interact with more empowered customers:

- It completes the seismic "shift of power" to consumers. They are enabled to influence all things and become co-owners of the brand.
- It is not about anonymous mass nor individual customers, but about individuals within a community, with influencers, creators, and consumers.
- It blurs the lines between marketing, sales, and service.
- It makes analytics and technology become critical enablers for real-time agility, flexibility, security, and repeatability, especially in industries like retail, hospitality, etc.

There is no "silver bullet" for formulating and executing a winning social media strategy; some of the leading players admit running a constant trial-and-error process through experimentation with social media.

However, experience shows that successful organizations are results oriented and instantly learn from their experience in order to rapidly adapt to consumer behaviors, their preferred communication preferences, and responses. Major shifts occurring at the intersection of consumers, marketers, and media are configuring the transition from an "economy of scale" to an "economy of target." Innovation in commercial strategies (format, pricing, targeting, and channel strategies) is the way ahead for new media companies. Management of analytics will be key in delivering value to advertisers. As Tom Peters, author of *In Search of Excellence*, said, "E-commerce is not a technology play. It's a relationship, partnering, communication, and organizational play, made possible by technology."

To reach this level of agility, leading organizations have embraced a new approach spanning across organization, tools, metrics, and analytics that allows them to iteratively learn, plan, engage, and measure business benefits from using social media to enable business objectives. The key is to monitor the web ecosphere—identify influencers, detractors, and competitors and target off-board channels. There is a constant need to listen—detect questions and conversation opportunities and then filter and prioritize opportunities. A constant engagement is needed by establishing presence, publishing content, and promoting incentives. And lastly, the need to collaborate across business functions (marketing, sales, customer service, HR, R&D, legal, etc.) and across geographical units (global/local) is key.

New Capabilities—Mobile Solutions: Think Process, Not Technology

The early bird may catch the worm, but
it's the second mouse gets the cheese.
—Unknown

Enterprise mobility is emerging as a key enabler across all aspects of an enterprise strategy, particularly as it makes its way to the inevitable "everywhere connectivity." The prevalence of high-speed data for mobile devices and the migration of many social media channels to mobile devices have resulted in significant uptake in consumer mobile use. This has been fueled by the relatively low cost of device acquisition due to telecom provider subsidies. In addition to standard phone usage, many of these consumers have grown accustomed to using their mobile device to access email, messenger, news, entertainment, weather, banking, and shopping price comparison information. These users embrace the new era of mobile technology and will gravitate toward service providers and employers that embrace it.

Mobile device usage has increased dramatically over the past few years, and use of smart phones is projected to grow dramatically over the coming years. Few can argue the merits and sheer market force of mobile technology. Already, more than one billion mobile devices are in use globally. The Yankee Group wireless survey indicates that 55 percent of large US businesses will deploy a wireless wide-area data solution by next year. The numbers are impressive. No matter which statistic strikes one as most compelling, the opportunity is enormous. With this many users and this much growth projected, companies are beginning to aggressively extend their products and services into the mobile space. The market is simply too promising for any company to stay out of the game.

A few years ago, acquisition and installation of a mobile application was challenging for many mobile device users. Now everyday users can find applications, buy them, install them, and provide user feedback, all from their device and with minimal effort. These mobile users now expect to leverage their mobile device to ease the activities of daily life and improve the way they conduct business. Mobile device usage will continue to grow at a dramatic pace in the coming years. According to industry researcher Gartner, there were more than twenty-eight million touchscreen smart phones purchased in North America in 2009. Gartner forecasts that this will continue to increase in the coming years, reaching over 123 million new touchscreen smart phones purchased in North America in the year 2013 (Gartner, "Forecast: Touchscreen Mobile Devices, Worldwide, 2006-2013," January 26, 2010).

Yet, the key to creating mobile business value is not in the technology itself, but in re-engineering key business processes for market-driven business change. Companies that thrive on these capabilities will be those that mold mobility into a standard capability and fundamentally transform the way commerce happens—not just work unplugged. Enterprises need to identify key foundation processes that can be mobilized across both horizontal and vertical lines of business. Pioneer companies, such as FedEx, UPS, etc., are adopting mobility and achieving hard benefits, including higher revenue, lower costs, faster time-to-market, and better customer service. The key benefits that companies seek:

> The key to creating mobile business value is not in the technology itself, but in re-engineering key business processes for market-driven business change.

- Increase employee productivity in the field
- Enhance enterprise information flow
- Maximize ROI on existing enterprise applications

Although technology continues to improve, there are still significant hurdles that must be overcome. The mobile ecosystem is a fragmented marketplace with no single end-to-end solution. The consumer is pushing mobile technology to enterprises based on the value mobility delivers to everyday life. Only with a thorough understanding of mobile technology and a complete business strategy will enterprises be able to realize the full potential of mobile solutions.

Concerns and Challenges with Mobile Solutions

There are many challenges with deploying a mobile solution, including cost to develop, security of data, usability and performance, and solution maintenance.

Cost/effort: The cost and effort to deploy a mobile solution can vary greatly depending on the functionality to deploy, the device platforms that will be supported, and the company's current back-office system implementation. In many cases the company already has a web-enabled application that can be extended to one or more mobile device types for substantially less than the cost to develop a new mobile solution.

Data security: Data privacy laws in the United States and in some other countries will make many companies wary of storing customer or policy data on a mobile device. Additionally, calculations and other data that are critical to some of the processes are proprietary, and the companies might be reluctant to put any of those data or calculations on the mobile device. There are proven mechanisms for securely storing this data in such a way; however, many companies will still be reluctant to deploy sensitive data to the mobile device.

Usability/performance: Usability of a system is important for all solutions. This is even more important for mobile solutions.

If the mobile application does everything that is required but is clumsy or confusing to use, then it will result in low user adoption. Also, if the user is stuck waiting on the application because of poor performance, then the user will not use the application. Over the past year, only four out of ten online mobile users were satisfied with their mobile experience, as per a survey by Forrester.

Solution maintenance: In addition to the cost to develop and deploy the mobile solution, there is also the added effort to maintain and support the solution. This requires having staff with the technical skills to update the solution as-needed, along with any additional hardware, software, and licensing costs associated with the solution. A key approach to minimizing the impact of this concern is to develop and deploy a mobile solution that naturally extends the company's existing IT infrastructure.

Identifying functionality: Establishing an enterprise mobile strategy is one of the most critical steps for a company to maximize return on investment (ROI). An enterprise mobile strategy is a road map that outlines their priorities, technology approach, benefits analysis for various functional solutions, and a prioritized list of initiatives for the carrier to implement. There are many approaches to deploying a mobile solution and many types of functionality that can be deployed to support the company and its industry-specific needs. Some examples of these objectives can be: increase consumer brand recognition, increase consumer leads and sales, improve agent productivity/sales tools, etc. For example, if a retail bank wants its customers to conduct bank transactions and deposit checks through their smart phones, they need to integrate this capability with existing systems and processes to build a robust mobile strategy. Each of these objectives would drive the creation of a different type of mobile solution.

There are a number of options for how to develop and deploy these mobile solutions. Defining the approach early allows future mobile work to extend previous work. This typically results in reduced future development effort and increased return on the previous development effort. For example, if a hotel chain wants to enable its customers to be able to walk into a hotel and have their smart phone automatically download the key to their room, then their value proposition of customer intimacy will dictate the mobile strategy.

Another important point for such solutions is that when deploying mobility solutions, all processes are not equal. To help executives better understand where and how mobility can improve the way they run their businesses, it is important to identify the processes to support business cases for driving the highest value. Based on the type of benefit and expected value,

> When deploying mobility solutions, all processes are not equal.

companies can categorize the processes to prioritize and tackle enterprise mobility:

- *Baseline*—Baseline processes are the foundations of mobility. They demonstrate a clear and hard business case for being mobilized in stand-alone fashion and do not depend on other business processes before they can demonstrate added value.
- *Support*—The next building blocks are support processes, which demonstrate business value when they are paired with the foundation built by a baseline process. They can be mobilized as a stand-alone process, but they will deliver the greatest value when combined with a baseline process.
- *Enabling*—Enabling processes enable additional functionality of another process, such as signature capture or printing.

- ***Unique***—Unique processes are those that provide substantial value to an organization if made mobile, but they are generally applicable only in specific industry segments and applications.

Of course, the categorization of a particular process will differ from industry to industry. Still, baseline processes are the fundamental drivers of value and can demonstrate benefits in a stand-alone fashion. Companies must start here, mobilizing a baseline process and using it as a basis to expand and launch other rollouts. Support, enabling, and unique processes may be mobilized along with a baseline process, providing for additional value streams. Companies are seeing significant, measurable impact deploying enterprise mobile solutions. Early and successful implementations demonstrate that productivity is the most significant value lever—having data at the point of activity speeds up activities, lowers costs, increases revenue, and provides new capabilities. Baseline processes, such as the ability for mobile workers to access customer data through a mobile device, are positively impacting business financials. For example, a utility company equipped its field work force with handheld mobile devices, thus eliminating ten minutes each technician spent on each ticket searching for a wired Internet connection to upload data. With forty thousand technicians, the company saved significant downtime and increased productivity.

There are companies that will deliver 5 percent greater labor productivity and up to a 30 percent reduction in working/fixed capital from optimized inventory levels and greater asset utilization. Reductions in indirect expenses, such as fewer support desk calls due to workers having direct, mobile access to knowledge data bases, can contribute a significant share of benefits from horizontal processes. Schedule and dispatch processes, which tend to be more expensive to implement, achieve payback in less than a year and are the easiest to justify with measurable hard benefits. Mobilizing vertical solutions for specific industry functions, such as utility field force enablement or package tracking, also provides important hard benefits—often at competitive survival levels. FedEx continues to upgrade its mobile solution suite with the latest innovations, shaving ten to twenty seconds off the delivery time for each of the 3.2 million parcels it delivers daily. Ford Motor Company implemented a mobile application to reduce waste in their fleet yards—a multi-million-dollar project with payback within nine months. Soft benefits also matter and are often regarded as substantial enough to justify an initial pilot. Customer service responsiveness helps increase customer satisfaction while mobile devices help employees feel more professional and productive.

In adopting mobility to solve business problems and re-engineer business processes, companies should consider the following steps:

- Identify key baseline processes that will extract unrealized value by modifying and mobilizing the process and justify with a business case.
- As a standard part of a complete enterprise strategy (rather than as a separate entity), consider mobility an enabler of core business processes.
- Create a mobile strategy—define technical standards and common mobility infrastructure. Understand, plan for, and address the potential risks of technology, networking, security, coverage, and bandwidth obstacles early in the planning process. Every part of IT should have a mobility component as needed.
- Concentrate on human performance—determine factors in some people embracing the technology while others resist it and learn how best to get people to adopt the change (as explained in chapter 3).

Despite advances in wireless technology and lowered device prices over the last several years, mobilizing business processes is still a difficult task. The mobile ecosystem is complex and fragmented with no single end-to-end solution, no single point of accountability, and no standardized approach, which makes for unclear responsibility. The required technology is evolving, although sometimes slowly; for example, 4G in the United States is available in only a few cities versus the national presence desired. Because pervasive network connectivity may not be available for years to come, enterprises with large field operations must make hard choices between enterprise mobile architectures and solutions. And robust operational procedures are needed to support the thousands of devices in the hands of mobile workers. Even with advances in mobile middleware software and device management, enterprises still need the competent knowledge of this evolving market to ensure successful implementations.

Human factors continue to influence how well mobility is adopted within an organization. At several enterprises, adoption was slow because workers were not comfortable with the technology. Some field force employees view mobility as a tool that monitors their daily activity, while sales force employees are often concerned about the image the physical appearance of the device denotes. Comprehensive change management helps enterprises better engage people components into mobile-enabled process change.

> Human factors continue to influence how well mobility is adopted within an organization.

New Capabilities— Cloud Computing

As organizations look at their business and IT capabilities, they are bombarded with advancements on the technology front— some disruptive and some gradual changes. Recently the industry is abuzz about cloud computing. A stock analyst said of technology companies, "If they ever say that their services are offered through the cloud, their stock is typically in the clouds." As the CEO of Salesforce.com, Marc Benioff, said in 2010, "The cloud services companies of all sizes. . . . The cloud is for everyone. The cloud is a democracy."

It is obvious to anyone that cloud computing turns computing costs into a variable cost rather than a fixed cost by providing compute capacity on demand. The two key technology enablers that have led to the adoption of the cloud are increased network bandwidth and infrastructure virtualization. But the narrow differences between the loosely related buzz words beg definition and clarity:

> Cloud computing turns computing costs into a variable cost rather than a fixed cost by providing compute capacity on demand.

- **Virtualization**—A set of technologies to create a virtual computing infrastructure by allowing division of physical assets (processing power, storage and network bandwidth) into virtual machines (e.g., VMware virtual server).
- **Elastic computing (EC)**—A technology for provisioning and load balancing that doles out the virtual infrastructure on demand (e.g., Amazon's EC2).
- **Grid computing (GC)**—A computing architecture in which a large number of individual computers work in parallel to solve a problem (e.g., Google's Map-Reduce).

- **Utility computing (UC)**—A business or pricing model in which the users of computing resources pay (only) for the resources they use.
- **Cloud computing**—Typically some combination of the above to provide a fluid pool of remote computing. It is "fluid" in the sense that computing can more readily be divided (virtualization), doled out on demand (EC), and combined. This is typically associated with a utility computing business model.

And the different types of cloud also need some definitions and clarity:

- *Private (internal) cloud:* Emulating the cloud computing on corporate datacenters and access through private networks. The assets are company owned, and the scope of computing capabilities is bounded by exclusive membership as defined by the company.
- *Public cloud:* Cloud computing in the traditional mainstream sense. An off-site third-party provider shares resources and bills on a fine-grained utility computing basis. The companies consuming these capabilities do not own the assets except data, and the scope is open to anyone who can pay for service as delivered by the provider.
- *Hybrid cloud:* Some resources are provided and managed inhouse and some others externally.

With all these different types of options, there is an emergence of companies that are acting as brokers of cloud services. Of course, this form of service intermediary, just like business relationship management (as explained in chapter 4), needs to manage providers, consumers, stakeholders, and other business relationships. But whether this happens slowly or at an enormous pace, the adoption of these cloud computing capabilities requires a number of technology and operational considerations:

- **SLAs**—Service levels agreed between provider and user on various fronts like uptime, backup, security, privacy, etc.
- **Legal**—Use of public cloud services may be restricted for certain business functions.
- **Open source**—If a cloud is based on open standards and software, a detailed study is necessary before adopting certain public cloud offerings.
- **Privacy**—Cloud is based on a shared environment, so privacy requirements have to be validated.
- **Governance**—This refers to the controls and processes that make sure policies are enforced.
- **Portability**—This is about the ability of moving components or systems between environments.
- **Integration**—With cloud computing, integrating various components and systems can be complicated by issues such as multi-tenancy, federations, and government regulations.
- **Interoperability**—This is very critical for a successful adoption of the cloud.
- **Sustainability**—This is more relevant to private cloud and is achieved through improved resource utilization, efficient processes, etc.
- **Security**—Currently security is a contentious issue, which seems to delay the widespread adoption of cloud computing in some places. Large investments are being made by many companies to develop a cloud security model. Organizations need to define the risks and how to manage them and figure out, "How much security do I need?" After that, the company needs to develop plans for effective and cost-efficient security controls.

When thinking from a business strategy perspective and about the impact to top and bottom lines, the questions to think about are as follows:

- How will companies react to the rise of new competitors built on the cloud "pay as you go" model? For example, can a new company start up with near-zero investments with a pay-per-use billing system and third party networks?
- Is it possible for my company to enter new markets using cloud solutions? Which opportunities make sense?
- How will I negotiate and partner with my IT vendors, if I can instantly switch my processing power from one to another?
- How will one global online marketplace modify the dynamics of relationship with customers for non-IT products and services?
- How will cloud computing require more aggressive movements against my competitors so I can benefit from first mover advantage?
- Will a faster time-to-market using cloud services allow a company to develop capabilities fast enough to make it more conservative in new business ventures?
- Can I offer any cloud-based solutions to my suppliers to expand my knowledge and control through the value chain?
- How can my IT vendors create competitive advantage for themselves through cloud? What should be my company position in order to not be harmed?

FOUR

Do Those Things Correctly

Efficiency is intelligent laziness.
—Unknown

Strategy is creating fit among a company's activities.
The success of a strategy depends on doing many things
well—not just a few—and integrating among them.
—Michael Porter, professor at Harvard Business School
and author of *Competitive Advantage*

The difficulty with information-based technologies is that they are seldom perceived as services by IT management, and hence are not designed and managed as services to customers. Instead, IT is often managed as administrative routines with internal efficiency and costs as the main criteria. Consequently, customers and business units see IT as an administrative unit rather than as a *service provider*. As we have seen all through this book, value emerges in the customers' consumption or usage of IT services in the pursuit of an outcome for themselves. Only when the service provider comprehends what is effective in facilitating those outcomes is it ready to apply internal efficiency measurements and effect process, technological, and organizational changes. Long-term success is a matter of identifying the outcomes that matter to the customer and making them visible while making those outcomes that are irrelevant either invisible or extinct.

This is all about **HOW** work should be done.

After we have looked at the above components to ensure that the IT organization is doing the right things (strategy and value targeting), we focus on doing those things right—focusing on the efficiency with which those initiatives should be executed. This is all about *HOW* work should be done.

The Hangzhou Bay Bridge, which connects two parts of eastern coastal China, is twenty-two miles in length and had a price tag of $1.7 billion. The local government approved plans and funding for the massive project, which would shorten the travel distance between Ningbo and Shanghai by seventy-five miles over water, but then what remained was the HOW—and they employed six hundred experts for nearly a decade before the final, successful design was reached. The bridge opened to the public in May 2008. Today, it is the longest trans-oceanic bridge in the world and is expected to last one hundred years. The HOW is critical.

To understand why this is an important function of the CIO's organization, it's interesting to see the surveys by professional bodies like the Standish Group, Robbins-Gioia, KPMG, and OASIG, which reveal a dismal picture. Some results from the Chaos report by the Standish Group found out the following:

- 31 percent of software projects were cancelled before completion.
- 52 percent of projects cost almost double the original budget estimates.
- Only 9 percent of projects were on-time and within budget.
- On average, over 50 percent of the effort of producing software went into testing.
- Over 50 percent of the costs associated with software were incurred after delivery.

Even though the numbers tended to improve with the latest reports, the top reasons found for project failures are still the same—lack of user input, incomplete requirements and specifications, changing requirements, and lack of executive support. Therefore, it is very important for the IT leadership to be thinking about how effective and streamlined the processes are within the IT organization—demand management, portfolio management, risks management, etc. They should be focused on how their solution delivery and resource management processes are working to provide services to the business. They should be focused on how their infrastructure operations are run and how they can get to utility models for the same. In broad categories, these processes include relationship management, demand management, systems development processes, portfolio management, resource management, and financial management.

Business Relationship Management (BRM)

The concept of service management came about from the work done in ITIL. (Information Technology Infrastructure Library is a registered trademark of the United Kingdom's Office of Government Commerce. It is a set of concepts and practices for IT services management, development, and operations.) The goal of BRM is to move away from multiple points of contact for the business for services defined and measured in technical terms. Historically, the IT organization used to service multiple users across multiple business units with day-to-day requests as well as medium-term change management work. The segmentation of the traditional IT department used to be utmost in operational domains—in-house and/or third party (e.g., email, network, servers, etc.). This led to their services having an IT/IS internal focus, random change management discplines, suboptimal IT/IS resource utilization, and poor cost control of service delivery.

The concept of service management is to break up the direct relationship between users of these IT operational domains by setting up a communication interface of the service provider. A clear distinction is typically made between a customer-facing organization and delivery organizations (projects and services)— ideally with a clear set of objectives, roles and accountabilities, and skills profile defined for each. The overall business relationship is owned by one customer-facing IT organization, which means that accountability for all IT projects and services sits with this BRM organization. Depending on the size of the IT organization, some of the functions of the BRM organization are as follows:

- *Customer services:* Customer services interacts with representatives of the customer groups on change management, service content, and service performance.

- *Domain management:* Domain management interacts with representatives of operational domains on the solution of specific user requests. The operational domains are teams (in-house or third party) that specialize in certain infrastructure or application areas and that perform the requested services. Examples are IT operations, IT services, or IT security.

- *Service control:* Service control interacts with users for day-to-day issue resolutions. The SLAs govern the relationship between users and customers on the one hand and customer services and service control on the other hand. The operating level agreements (OLAs) govern the relationship between the operational domains on the one hand and domain management on the other hand.

Figure 26: Why Business Relationship Management

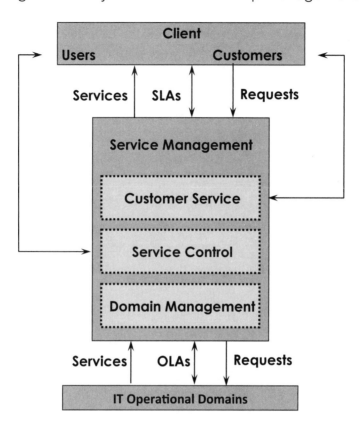

The objective is to manage IT as a business and establish relationships with customers (internal) so as to deliver better service at lower cost. The service needs to be defined, measured, and reported on in business terms, and the work needs to be driven by service requirements. The goal to drive the service delivery performance upwards is through SLAs to set and manage expectations, service level measurement, and performance management to enable efficiency improvements. The goal to drive costs down is achieved by establishing an SLA fee structure to encour-

> The objective is to manage IT as a business and establish relationships with customers (internal) so as to deliver better service at lower cost.

age standardization and charging premium prices for customized and nonstandard services across the organization. This function also matches demand and value by chargeback mechanisms to link service cost to business value being delivered. The cost visibility of service delivery through transparent pricing helps regulate value in demand and supply of services.

The role of this organization is to manage the relationship with business functions, ensure service delivery and improvement, maximize value from existing investments, identify business IT innovations, and provide business analysis. The activities include engagement planning, business–IT strategic planning, issue and escalation management, IT performance reporting, and so on. In such a setting, the service provider identifies and documents the stakeholders and customers of the services. The service provider and customer typically attend a service review to discuss any changes to the service scope, SLAs, or contracts (if present). The service provider should also have a named individual or individuals who are responsible for managing customer satisfaction and the whole business relationship process. A process should be defined for obtaining and acting upon feedback from regular customer satisfaction measurements. In many organizations, the project management office (PMO) has begun to manage the demand and supply aspect of the IS functions. This elevates the PMO role from being operation-based and tactical to a more strategic role. They need to be staffed by skilled resources that can create the necessary impact. The IT PMO becomes the "Front Office," coordinating (among other things) the impact assessment of demand across IT, as explained below.

1. The business unit submits a "brief" for change initiative in consultation with the IT relationship manager—to validate that the demand is aligned and properly constituted.
2. The IT "Front Office" supports the relationship manager by collating and validating all briefs and circulates these

for impact assessment to affected internal and external domains.

3. External service providers or delivery owners assess impact—for example, xx days to help with business case, between yy-zz days for implementation. Impacts are broken down across predefined resource pools—for example, project managers, analysts, etc.

4. The Front Office collates impacts and establishes a "heat-map" of change impact across service lines and resource pools. They then allocate resource pool capacity across the delivery service lines—and monitor subsequent resource utilization.

5. Service line schedulers manage day-to-day resource needs within allocated limits.

Guiding Principles for Business Relationship Management

- IT services should be packaged and defined in business terms (description, features, service levels, pricing). Business clients should be able to easily understand what they are buying or why they are paying for something.

- Unit pricing of IT services should be based on business controls/levers. Pricing based on business oriented controls/levers (e.g., pricing based on number of users, number of transactions, hours of service, etc.) provides the business users the ability to control overall IT costs. Initial pricing may only provide limited "levers" to the business.

- Component costs should drive the IT service price. The total price for an IT service should be the sum of all of the IT component costs.

> Business clients should be able to easily understand what they are buying or why they are paying for something.

- IT services or components should be designed to facilitate easy comparison and benchmarking with third party service providers.
- IT services and components should drive IT fulfillment processes. IT must be able to rapidly, effectively, and efficiently deliver IT services to customers. Improving IT service price/performance is grounded in improving IT process performance.
- IT services and components should drive IT funding and functional budgets. Customers should be charged for IT services (pricing)—this is the IT funding mechanism. The component cost structure within an IT service will drive IT functional budgets. This is explained in chapter 3.

Governance

What is a committee? A group of the unwilling,
picked from the unfit, to do the unnecessary.
—Richard Harkness, American radio and TV journalist

G overnance is the creation of an ecosystem in which others can *manage effectively*—this is how decisions are made, sponsored, enforced, and the results tracked. The goal of this function is to make sure that the alignment issues that were decided with the business actually get done at strategic, operational, and tactical levels. IT governance is the decision-making process and its impact on the IT organization's ability to meet its objectives, and it is a foundation for realizing business value from IT investments. IT organizations require mature IT governance, that is, effectiveness in decision making and efficiency in operations.

> Governance is how decisions are made, sponsored, enforced, and the results tracked.

How are decisions ***made***—Who plays what role in the decision making? What processes are used? How are investments authorized? How does leadership work for IT and ***sponsor*** the right decisions? Who is the "evangelist" for IT? How is joint ownership secured?

What is measured and by whom to ***enforce*** those decisions made? What incentive system is used? What accountabilities and authorities exist? How are investments managed? What knowledge is required to ***ensure the correctness*** of decision making? How is a fresh view injected? How do we learn continuously?

There is widespread debate in the industry as to how governance should be laid out, because a lot of the success in converting strategies to execution is about planning and discipline, both of which are subsets of a broader governance function. The quote from Charles Handy in *Harvard Business Review* (April 2009) sums it up:

> Today the management, monitoring, and governance of a business are increasingly seen as separate functions to be done by separate bodies, even if some of the membership of those bodies overlaps. This is the corporate equivalent of the separation of powers. Management is the *executive function*, responsible for delivering the goods. Monitoring is the *judicial function*, responsible for seeing that the goods are delivered according to the laws of the land, that standards are met, and ethical principles observed. Governance is the *legislative function*, responsible for overseeing management and monitoring and, most important for the corporation's future, for strategy, policy, and direction.

The structures, processes, and tools and metrics for IT governance flow from the corporate level. By considering both the *rate of industry change* and the *company basis for competitive advantage*, executives can understand how the organization's IT governance function adds value. While considering industry/company rate of change, you need to look at pace of change dependent on the industry that the company operates in. These are driven by factors such as rapid shifts in customer needs, disruptive changes, product/service offerings, etc.

If there is a rapid rate of change in the industry, the key to competitive advantage will be innovation. In such an environment, developing an IT organization that is flexible to accommodate rapidly changing business strategies and requirements is important. The company needs to foster an innovation culture to create innovative IT-enabled business models and business capabilities through a combination of existing and emerging technologies and deliver the innovative capabilities to capture first-mover advantages. But if the industry is slow changing (e.g., airlines, manufacturing, etc.), then meeting business needs while supporting low-cost orientation becomes the governance guiding principle. Keep costs low, minimize changes, maximize lifecycles of IT assets, and leverage cost-saving devices (e.g., shared services, co- sourcing, outsourcing, etc.)—these become the themes of such an organization.

The company's basis for competitive advantage can be either improving operational efficiency by minimizing costs or optimizing the existing business model or differentiation through products or service. IT governance depends on how the business itself is structured. There are three traditional organizational models for structuring IT within an organization:

- *Centralized IT*: The business linkage is dictated.
- *Decentralized IT*: IT functions are moved into the business to ensure linkage.
- *Federal IT*: A hybrid model, where shared services are overlaid on either previous model with enterprise leadership. This model is generally seen to build upon the strengths of both the centralized and decentralized models.

Governance Structures

The IT governance structures are organizational components of how IT will interact with business functions. To maximize performance results, the IT organization structure should be tailored to the business context and operating objectives. Most organizations will likely require a combination of organizational models applied to specific organization units.

As discussed above, depending on where the company is in its operative objective, structures, and environment, the governance models will vary—it could be top management only, team based with

> To maximize performance results, the IT organization structure should be tailored to the business context and operating objectives.

committees for specific centers of excellence, or completed federated for dealing with rapid industry change.

The right structure helps all IT initiatives to be aligned to business initiatives that enable the company level and business level objectives. IT investments and initiatives align with the architecture standards unless the value of an alternative is much greater. Common IT processes and assets are utilized as the established default to achieve asset optimization.

As depicted in the following figure and explained in the text, the various stakeholders involved in governance need to be adjusted according to the needs of the company, its industry, and its place vis-à-vis its competition.

Figure 27: Governance Structures for IT Organizations

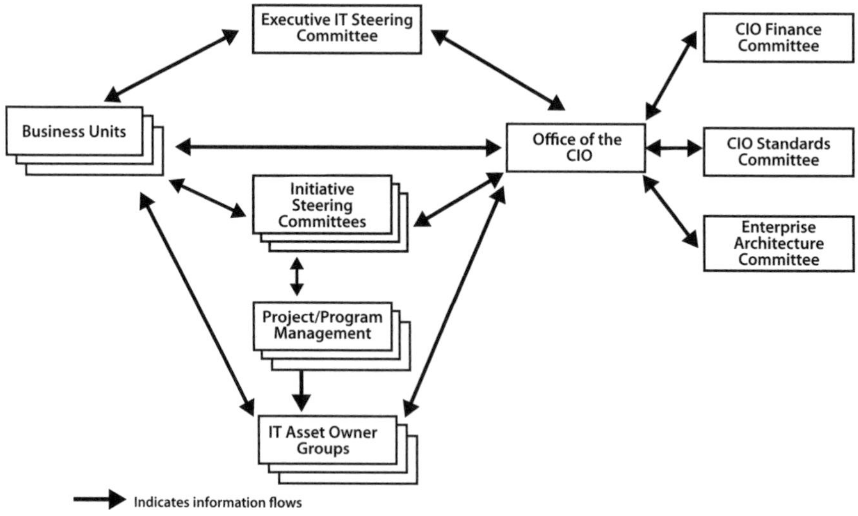

Indicates information flows

- **IT steering committee**—This group is there to resolve critical IT performance issues and cross-functional project delivery issues and be able to allocate and approve IT budgets in terms of discretionary and nondiscretionary spending.

- **Business unit leadership**—This group is responsible for day-to-day management of business functions (examples in an insurance industry would be underwriting, claims, collections, finance, etc.). It determines department priorities and identifies potential projects and enhancements. They are also responsible for escalating business-critical service level or IT performance issues.
- **IT leadership committee**—This group is responsible for day-to-day management of IT operations. They create and manage approved IT budgets, manage resources, and monitor progress on approved projects.
- **Architecture and standards**—This group takes business applications and IT infrastructure standardization decisions to the IT steering committee as needed. They identify the impact of proposed and approved projects on the environment and set technology standards in line with business priorities.
- **Project/program steering committee**—This group is actively involved in escalating scope/budget issues and also reviews project status, specifically "red lights" in the execution of the program or projects.

IT Governance Processes

1. IT Annual Planning

Developing an IT annual plan involves addressing questions across five perspectives in a phased approach. As shown below, the phased approach should be of establishing the vision, assessing the current situation, planning for a future state, and finally executing or implementing the plan. In each of these phases multiple perspectives need to be coherently tied up—business impact, investment and value realization, architecture of systems, change programs needed, and delivery skills needed.

Figure 28: Strategic Planning for IT Organizations

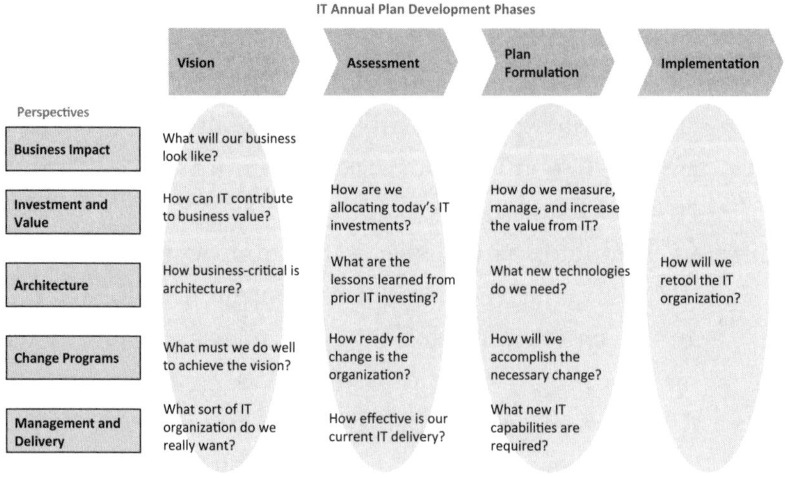

IT Annual Plan Development Phases

Perspectives	Vision	Assessment	Plan Formulation	Implementation
Business Impact	What will our business look like?			
Investment and Value	How can IT contribute to business value?	How are we allocating today's IT investments?	How do we measure, manage, and increase the value from IT?	
Architecture	How business-critical is architecture?	What are the lessons learned from prior IT investing?	What new technologies do we need?	How will we retool the IT organization?
Change Programs	What must we do well to achieve the vision?	How ready for change is the organization?	How will we accomplish the necessary change?	
Management and Delivery	What sort of IT organization do we really want?	How effective is our current IT delivery?	What new IT capabilities are required?	

The team needs to assess the company's current positioning—industry, marketplace, regulatory environment, capabilities and skills, and culture. It needs to then determine the vision for the company for the next twelve months and beyond—define the overarching corporate strategy into capabilities, translate vision into a discrete set of goals (financial, operational, and strategic), and identify constraints. This leads to definition of capability gaps and refining of IT strategic plans and actions. The team can then finalize the plan and corresponding budget and approve the same. It should then create a set of metrics to measure performance. Corporate executives often ask about how often to revisit these processes and when reprioritization should occur based on external and internal events. The answer will depend on the rate of change in the industry and any major shocks to the ecosystem.

Most organizations have a plan for providing long-term guidance for their brand—three-year objectives. This follows one-year tactics and milestones by quarter, and in this annual planning organizations define business unit actions and interdependencies. They define these one-year actions by month to drive actions/milestones to individual actions of business units in order to clarify accountability and track progress. The direction remains stable for some time, although annual plans might be changed for short-term recalibration of the tactics and operations. As Mark Nadler from Oliver Wyman wrote (July 2011), "Any genuine shift in strategy implies a change in emphasis—it might involve different customers or markets, new technologies or business processes, unfamiliar leadership styles or management techniques." In fact, Publilius Syrus said in the first century BC, "It is a bad plan that admits of no modification." A senior executive in a company recently said,

> We have established that our strategic plan should not change too often. Typical planning horizon is three to five years. We then do big building blocks that we call these vital few objectives—VFOs—with targets like increase sales, add new customers, grow sales to existing customers, etc. Next we define the initiatives that support those VFOs. These are one year or less in duration and are getting to the specific tasks that need to be done. Finally, we build a quarterly plan that acts as our road map for the quarter.

Reminds one of this dialogue in *Alice in Wonderland* by Lewis Carroll:

Alice: What a funny watch! It tells the day of the month, and it doesn't tell what o'clock it is!

The Hatter: Why should it? Does your watch tell you what year it is?

Alice: Of course not, but that's because it stays the same year for such a long time together.

The Hatter: . . . which is just the case with mine.

2. Plan and Prioritize Initiative Portfolio

This sub-process helps create a consolidated view of all demand types to realize tradeoffs and synergies. It helps establish objective and repeatable criteria that people agree to and understand. It also leads to reduction in the subjectivity of project approval and prioritization. The team can take the results of the IT prioritization process and begin adding projects in priority order to the IT consolidated plan. If needs to ensure that project dependencies are considered when adding the prioritized projects and fill the IT consolidated plan to the target budget levels. This might involve iterating through and driving to greater levels of detail in terms of resource requirements and staffing requirements to manage the proverbial project funnel. The IT steering committee should look at the project to see the constraints and the balance of benefits and risks before approving, rejecting, or holding projects in the pipeline.

After some initial analysis and categorization, IT relationship managers or demand managers should focus on better prioritization. The project prioritization could be based on the following parameters:

- **Strategic Fit**

  The first aspect is to understand the *business strategic fit*: What value discipline is the organization pursuing—customer intimacy, operational excellence, or product leadership? This will enable the stakeholders to understand whether they need to focus on things like partnerships, enabling or acquiring new product capability, or reducing cost and complexity, etc. The second aspect is to understand the *IT strategic fit*: aligning the IT strategy to a corporate value discipline could mean that the IT organization will understand where to focus—systems that enable faster delivery in the future, or reducing IT running costs and risk through standardization, or building new architected capability, etc. For example, if a commercial bank is acquired by some retail bank, it should start looking at improving its CRM capabilities.

- **Business Value**

  The governance process probes into what the project's payback is: Will it take twelve months or eighteen months to break even? What is the NPV of the proposed initiative? Especially with today's economic climate, companies are putting even very high NPV projects on hold to minimize initial cash outflow.

- **Risk**

  The governance team needs to assess the level of internal risk and external risk involved. It needs to understand the likelihood that the risk will occur and the magnitude in cash terms of these risks—value at risk. It needs to assess the *business value risk*—this assesses the potential for the proposed project to deliver the intended strategic benefit or the opportunity cost (the cost of not proceeding). It needs to also look at *architecture risk*—this assesses the risk associated with introducing new or changing technology into the current environment. What is the level of technology risk? Is there a need for a one-purpose technology solution that does not fit with the enterprise architecture? And lastly, it needs to look at *project implementation risk*—this assesses the likelihood that the proposed project will adhere to the planned scope and implementation time line. After these analyses the team also needs to ask: What are the risk response strategies—avoidance, transfer, mitigation?

- **Complexity**

  This team needs to see if the project is using very new technologies and if they have the skills to take on this initiative to build and support the new technology stack. It needs to understand if the company has the commitment and sponsorship to take on this project.

3. Realize Program/Project Benefits

This consists of execution of projects to achieve planned objectives, time frames, expenditure levels, and specific quality assurance levels. The team needs to develop comprehensive programs and project plans that maintain alignment to business needs, are accepted by the business, and mitigate delivery risk. The established business metrics should be monitored to implement a benefit realization mechanism to measure the outcomes achieved.

4. Manage IT Asset Portfolio

This consists of identifying, assessing, and administering proposed changes to assets (including applications). The team needs to maintain integrity of assets and ongoing alignment with business direction throughout asset lifecycle. This aspect is explained in elaborate detail in chapter 5.

5. Develop and Measure Performance Metrics

The governance team also needs to manage an ongoing process to measure the performance of business–IT initiatives and assets against established business goals. It needs to manage IT performance and drive continuous improvement through measures and incentives.

6. Establish and Manage Standards

The governance team needs to maintain the integrity and value of IT assets and initiatives through defined standards (architecture, processes, and policies). It needs to document and deploy relevant standards for business solution delivery, operations, and performance management. The architectural team that is represented in this team needs to evaluate and recommend potential changes to existing standards.

7. Develop IT Operating Budget

The governance team needs to develop and administer IT operating budgets to achieve operational efficiency goals. It has to establish and maintain IT resources and funding levels commensurate with lines of businesses and clients' requirements.

8. Manage Service Providers

The governance team needs to manage service provider relationships, contracts, and delivery levels and optimize service provider utilization across lines of businesses (LoBs).

Demand Management—Splitting Demand from Supply

Never put off till tomorrow what you can avoid altogether.
—Sinclair Lewis, American author, Nobel laureate for literature

One of the biggest IT challenges is to institutionalize IT demand management processes in the correct manner. IT demand management is a process to *receive* adequate initiative requests, *evaluate* these requests for ROI and alignment, *prioritize* them, and hence create the right IT services organization by proper *service catalog management*. The value proposition of such a process is that it reduces investment risk, optimizes resource utilization, and minimizes cross-functional inefficiencies. It helps to focus resources on high-value business needs through more accurate forecasts. It instills in the organization a greater discipline for developing realistic business cases that capture total cost and return on investment to enable trade-off decisions. This helps the IT organization to step over its proverbial keep-the-lights-on role and engage more in EPS-enhancing partnerships with the business.

It's important to realize that, depending on the IT structure within the firm, this can be less challenging or just an excruciating exercise. Part of the IT demand management culture is embedded in an overlying umbrella of IT governance. This includes governance **processes** (processes that enable effective decisions and management of IT through all stages of planning, delivering, and operating), goals and **metrics** (business performance objectives and measures that provide insight and guidance to both business and IT leadership), and governance **structure** (culture, structures, and responsibilities that are

This includes governance *processes*, goals and *metrics*, and governance, structure.

clear, efficient, and aligned with achieving the business objectives). The process for setting the right structure for IT demand management is to set up a structure for receiving, framing, prioritizing, confirming, and base-lining the initiatives undertaken by the IT organization. Part of the *receiving* phase is establishing an initiative triage and classification mechanism to help look at what might bring the best bang for the buck.

Initiative Request Triage and Classification

During the initial phases the team needs to be looking at elements like enterprise architecture alignment, business case development, impact analysis, and portfolio allocation. This is to ensure that the right stakeholders are enabled to capture the business and IT needs and that everyone is looking at a bifocal strategy with tradeoffs for short-term tactical projects and long-term strategic initiatives. For the IT steering committee (ideally a team of both business and IT participants) to look at the initiatives, the IT organization can create thresholds for requests that they'll look at, depending on the size and industry of the firm. For example:

- Initiatives that are more than three months in duration
- Initiatives that have an initial capital outlay of more than $150,000
- Initiatives with cross-functional business impacts

This process helps minimize effort focused on non-value-adding project requests such as:

- Small enhancements that have no impact within the system and are less than forty hours of effort to design, code, and test
- Requests that require immediate action, have no impact within the system, entail low complexity, and involve less than eight hours of effort

- A request for a new report or updated report from the data warehouse (this does not include reports from specific systems [e.g., adhoc or focus reports])
- Functionality in the system that is not working as designed (e.g., any kind of help desk ticket)

> Another important aspect of demand management is that it is an *iterative and continuous process.*

Another important aspect of demand management is that it is an *iterative and continuous process.* There should be a mechanism set to monitor this continually for performance management, status tracking, and corrective action planning.

Program Management

Only Robinson Crusoe had everything done by Friday.
—Unknown

The program management office (PMO) is a centralized unit of the leadership team dedicated to program management activities. A new, more sophisticated way of managing is needed to match the complexity of the comprehensive change programs that are being undertaken by organizations. Many organizations have adopted program management as a way of managing this complexity. Perhaps the most compelling driving force is the bottom line result. Program management addresses the causes of program failures in order to make the program successful.

Figure 29: What is Program Management?

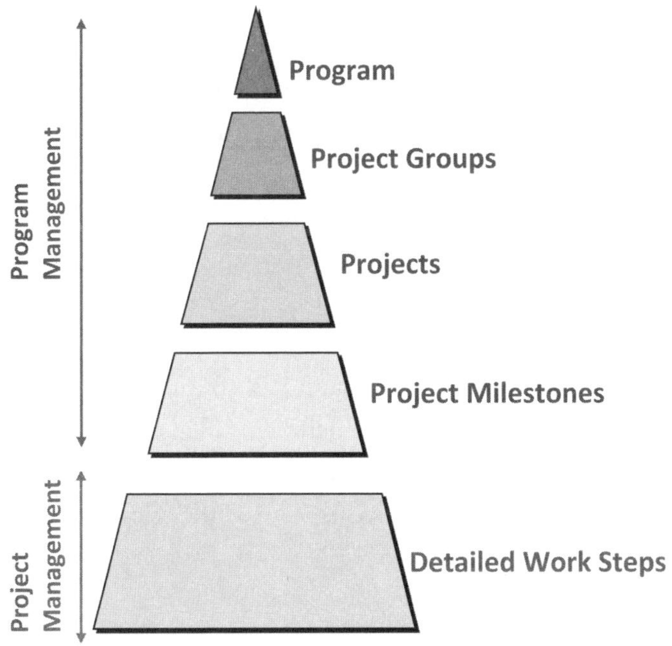

Project Additions

Part of strategic program management function is to be able to manage the demand of projects accordingly to some objective rationale—please refer to chapter 4 on demand management. Part of the PMO role is to be able to verify the relevance of new project additions to the PMO and compile standard project documentation. This requires a good understanding of the goals and expectations for the initiatives. It also involves scoring projects based on objective, quantifiable evaluation criteria and ranking the project requests by their weighted scores. When prioritizing project candidates, one can use the decision analysis and resolution (DAR) technique. DAR is a structured and formalized process that helps organize decision making when complicated issues with a variety of possible answers exist. The team has to assess the impact and the interdependency of new projects for inclusion in PMO and develop documentation for new projects.

Interdependency Management

One of the most important functions of the PMO team is to manage the various interdependencies in a program. Often the projects are being run by different teams. In many organizations the sub-components of a program even report to different business units and different leaders within the company. Managing the dependencies and the schedule becomes very complex when the sense of urgency and the vision of the end state is different in different units. The PMO team has to proactively identify and resolve project interdependencies in collaboration with the concerned projects. The team needs to constantly develop and monitor action plans to resolve interdependencies and escalate where necessary.

Value Management/Benefits Realization

One of the critical roles of a strategic PMO is to manage the value achievement of the initiatives. It needs to ensure sponsor and executive ownership of the business case. Not all stakeholders or sponsoring organizations are interested in creating a business case. The business case and tracking benefits allow the stakeholders in IT projects to jointly address their key concerns with project investments. Finance stakeholders want to know if the money is being spent wisely. Business stakeholders want to know if they will see the benefits they expected. IT stakeholders are interested in whether they are receiving what was promised.

Issue Management

The PMO has to resolve program-level issues in a timely and effective manner, which involves assessment and detailing of issues, development and monitoring of action plans to resolve issues, and escalating issues when necessary. Issues management requires that the company listen to customer's concerns, review and monitor projects, fix problems, escalate concerns, and provide corrective activity as required, as well as communicate results to all concerned stakeholders.

Risk Management—Plan for risks, respond to issues

Risk is an uncertain circumstance or event that could stand in the way of achieving an objective. Risk management is not about being risk averse but about establishing an iterative process for responding to variations from expected outcomes. An issue refers to a problem involving a significant choice between two or more alternatives for an event that is happening *now*. Since an issue has already been realized, it can no longer be mitigated and must instead be resolved. An issue might adversely affect a request/release's budget, quality, schedule, performance, system service, or system design. Risk describes situations that could occur in the future.

> The goal of risk management is to focus attention on minimizing threats to the achievement of project objectives.

A risk can be mitigated so that it is not realized. When a risk is realized, it becomes an issue. The goal of risk management is to focus attention on minimizing threats to the achievement of project objectives. The relationship with other management processes—such as quality management, issue management, or status reporting—is important. The team has to provide an organized approach for the following:

- Identifying and assessing risks and the details on impact
- Having plans for dealing with a potential risk and minimizing its probability of occurring
- Determining cost-effective risk reduction actions
- Monitoring and reporting progress on the action plan to reduce risk

Change Management

Part of the change management is to make sure that the program as a whole is achieving the benefits that were decided upon in the beginning of the initiative. But this also tries to ensure that if there are changes in the direction, strategies, or conditions of the business, then the project is able to be re-calibrated to ensure it still stands to achieve the benefits needed by the initiative.

The next steps are for the team to identify project change and understand all the alternatives and solutions. The team needs to understand the details and impact of the requested change, whether it involves scope, time lines, or cost. And most of the situations involve highlighting the interdependencies, since one change can affect many areas of the program. After authorization from stakeholders and proper logging of this change request, the PMO then needs to develop action plans to manage these program-level changes. As progress is made upon the changes, the PMO needs to prepare progress reports for the appropriate stakeholders and make sure the value realization piece of this change is captured adequately.

Progress Reporting

The PMO team needs to systematically monitor and report program progress, gather timely progress from projects, and consolidate project updates to produce program-level progress reports for the steering committee. This is the typical role that the PMO team plays in most organizations. But as explained above, the role of a PMO organization needs to be more strategic than just this function.

Communication Management

Needless to say, the PMO team needs to communicate relevant messages to the program stakeholders and coordinate communication with the team. Development and dissemination of program-level communication plans are much-needed functions, and the PMO team needs to be very proactive in this area—as they say, "You can never over-communicate."

Communication will not always be a matter of life and death, but it can be in some situations. Researchers found that communication was the primary factor in Vietnam-era prisoners of war preventing the widespread psychological breakdown common among POWs during the Korean war, where little communication existed between prisoners. Prisoners in Vietnamese camps used any methods at their disposal to communicate with each other, and this often tipped the balance toward survival. Senator John McCain was shot down over Hanoi and kept prisoner for five and a half years, and he has stated, "As far as this business of solitary confinement goes, the most important thing for survival is communication with someone, even if it's only

> You can never over-communicate.

a wave or a wink, a tap on the wall, or to have a guy put his thumb up. It makes all the difference."

Another example demonstrates how some forms of communication help with results in a company. The CEO of a mid-size company elected a small core group that worked to tap into and unleash the "Green Champions" passion for making an energy efficiency culture at work. The aim for this group was to "show by doing."

This group engaged in what they called the "Switch-off Blitz"; after hours, the group assembled and went through every floor and checked every workstation to ensure that computers and monitors were switched off. Everyone who had done the right thing was rewarded with a note from the "green ninja" saying "Well done" and a block of fair trade chocolate. Those who had not switched off their computers properly received a note saying, "No chocolate for you—the green ninja is not happy." The energy monitoring system recorded a significant drop in energy consumption following the switch-off blitz that has been maintained. It's a great example of how an informal communication mechanism can make a difference.

Build vs. Buy—Strategic Sourcing

Delegating work works, provided the one delegating works too.
—Robert Half, American business man

More and more CIOs and sourcing managers today deal with pressures from executives to outsource IT services and see how the cost effectiveness factor plays in. But companies that establish sourcing relationships in piecemeal fashion fail to harness the synergies across the enterprise. Often, urgency to get the deal done leads buyers to myopically focus on price or only short-term value and consummate deals in a piecemeal fashion. Many buyers are unable to describe enterprise-wide expectations of service, cost implications, and the potential business benefits of sourcing arrangements. As a result, users fail to spend enough time reviewing the details of services being offered and cannot assess the objectives and specific definitions of services being provided. Providers remain vague about specific activities, functions, and performance measures to be monitored and reported, and the relationships between buyers and providers become adversarial. One of the outsourcers from a Fortune 500 company said,

> Companies that establish sourcing relationships in piecemeal fashion fail to harness the synergies across the enterprise.

The "three bids and a cloud of dust" mentality of old will not sustain us in today's market. We must be more disciplined and knowledgeable in our sourcing methods if we are to achieve savings. Depending on the design of the supply chain, our sourcing activities can permeate into just about every corner of our organization. For example, business process outsourcing (BPO) in logistics, manufacturing, IT, and HR requires us

> The IT organization can deliver the best mix of internally and externally sourced IT services that improve its ability to deliver against the business strategy.

to know how to procure or acquire an external solution through cross-functional effort.

The primary question is moving from "whether an organization owns or leases its technology" to "how the IT organization can deliver the best mix of internally and externally sourced IT services that improve its ability to deliver against the business strategy." Sourcing strategy develops the guiding principles for change based on the business strategy and vision, and it leverages multiple, optimum mixes of external and internal sources for execution.

The key question in making the sourcing decisions is: "How ready are the company's IT capabilities to support the business strategy?" What are the drivers prompting companies to examine sourcing in today's business world? What are the *financial drivers*—is it cost containment or cutbacks, balance between costs, quality, and service, or limited capital funds? What are the *business drivers*—is it growing business demands, efficiency and effectiveness imperatives, service credibility with business, focus on core competencies, or simply time to market for business solutions? What are the *management drivers*—time to market or simply own or lease services? What are the *capability drivers*—need for economies of scale, existing poor performance, or the inability to develop or re-skill personnel? When making a sourcing decision, what are the key considerations?

- **Strategic importance**—Key consideration needs to be given to the relative impact of a service area on the company's revenues and overall profitability. Executives need to determine how strategic the function is to their organization currently and how it fits into their future plans.

- **Current capability**—Executives need to see the relative strength of a service area's technical and business know-how, processes, and tools. They need to see what the capabilities of the function are and how those capabilities compare to the requirements.
- **Ownership preference**—Executives need to understand the relative preference of management to own, share, or transfer out IT assets based on company beliefs, values, and sourcing experience. They need to see how easily the function can be transitioned to another sourcing strategy.

Depending on the operating model of a company and how central its IT organization is, the IT sourcing decisions need to be consolidated into a framework where the organization classifies suppliers based on their relative importance to the company's operations. It then engages suppliers in collaborative, continual cost improvements and value creation within the company's supply chain and provide a factual basis, with supporting evidence, for managing supplier performance. The IT organization needs to define a supplier classification strategy so it can determine which suppliers are most critical to operations. The *strategic suppliers* are ones that provide the greatest potential value to the company and pose the highest potential risk of impacting delivery to customers. The focus should be on partnering on opportunities with these suppliers (e.g., beta testing software, advisory councils, etc.). The next tier, *key suppliers*, is the set of suppliers that are essential to daily operations, but the relationship is managed more operationally/ tactically. They possess potential to be high-value business partners in the future, and the focus should be on risk and performance. The last tier, *non-core suppliers*, is a set of suppliers that are deemed to be lower value or are not critical to operations and are managed primarily through tactical sourcing efforts, with minimal time required to manage the supplier relationship.

Once sourcing decisions have been established, prior to the implementation of some kind of supplier relationship management solution, supplier performance metrics need to be defined to measure the success of each relationship. In order to measure success, suppliers need to be measured against performance metrics deemed important by the company's IT procurement—variables like responsiveness, satisfaction, SLA adherence, total spend, innovation, etc. The appropriate performance metrics to measure and the frequency of measuring will depend on the type and classification of the supplier.

The current trend for both application and infrastructure outsourcing is that companies are opting for a "best of breed" approach to partnering. More and more companies are segmenting their IT portfolio and selecting providers that best meet the needs of each specific segment. Consequently, service providers are seeing a reduction in the average size of outsourcing deals. As an example, in 1998, Bank One executives hammered out a $2 billion IT outsourcing deal with IBM and AT&T. Called the *Technology One* alliance, it was heralded as a groundbreaking partnership that would not only help Bank One cut costs but also increase innovation and market share. Everyone was excited. By 2002, both the agreement and the partnership were falling apart. Bank One was describing the contract as vague and refusing to pay for improvements necessary to make the deal work. Just three years into the contract, Bank One pulled the plug. Other mega outsourcing deals were careening toward similar fates. Companies are trying to build the tradeoff between multi-sourcing and getting too much of their portfolio in one basket. They are looking for core strengths that outsourcing companies can provide.

So the IT organization should develop sourcing strategies that encompass all business and IT portfolios across the enterprise to facilitate identification of advantageous sourcing groups and paths. The outcome will identify those businesses and IT processes that should be sourced together and those that should pursue separate sourcing paths.

- **Insource**—The company maintains control internally (usually for reasons of intellectual property, privacy, or strategic responsiveness). These are typically transformation projects with little or no ongoing service provider involvement. From the IT organization's standpoint, strong client management is required for long-term success.

- **Staff augmentation**—This is a strategy to save money while maintaining responsibility for application support and maintenance activities. Selective outsourcing/resourcing is leveraged, and the service provider acts as integrator of the systems.

- **Strategic alliance**—In this model, the service provider supplies complete staffing to support the targeted processes and functions. The company is able to leverage external cost structure benefits and expertise but still maintain an appropriate level of control.

- **Outsource**—In this model, the company delegates IT (or selected functions therein) to an external organization for which it is a core competency. This involves a dramatic change in culture and working practices. There is often a requirement for the client to invest in the personnel transition to manage HR issues.

Methodology—CMM, Agile, Waterfall, Six Sigma, et al.

I guess the importance of methodology can be illustrated by the following facetious story I heard somewhere: A mechanical engineer, a systems engineer, and a software engineer are in a car driving down a steep mountain road when the brakes fail. The driver desperately pumps the brake pedal, trying to control the speeding vehicle around cliff-edge bends, while the passengers do their best not to panic. The car finally hurtles toward a haystack, where it eventually grinds to a surprisingly safe stop. The three engineers all get out, shaken and relieved, and they take turns assessing the situation. "Hmm," says the mechanical engineer. "It looks like a brake line was leaking—let's repair the split, bleed the brakes, and we should be able to get on our way." The systems engineer thinks for a while and says, "Maybe we need to contact the manufacturer and the dealer to confirm exactly what the problem is." The software engineer slowly climbs into the driver's seat and, gesturing for the others to join him, says, "How about we get back on the road and see if it happens again?"

Since the start of the information technology age, *software quality* has been an ambiguous term, meaning different things to different people. It has been defined *internally* from the viewpoint of software developers, and it has been defined *externally* from the viewpoint of end users of the software. But either way, early in the history of software development it was obvious that software development could not be done in an ad hoc manner but needed to be subject to rules and methodologies to deliver a product or service that had attributes like robustness, correctness, adaptability, reusability, maintainability, etc.

Over the last couple of years, numerous software development methodologies have been introduced to guide development teams in achieving these quality goals. These methodologies have evolved from very disciplined processes like capability maturity model (CMM), waterfall, etc., to processes for high-speed, quick-to-market software development like behavior driven development (BDD), extreme programming (XP), SCRUM, etc.

But one thing is for sure: no matter which process or methodology is applied, the bottom line is that there is an impact of software processes on the software quality factors. One has to sit back and ask oneself these questions:

> No matter which process or methodology is applied, the bottom line is that there is an impact of software processes on the software quality factors.

- Is a process necessary to achieve software quality? Which aspects of software processes improve or hinder quality?
- How do we prioritize the quality factors and align the software processes based on these quality factors?
- What lessons have been learned from industrial experiences on method-based software development?

Since the inception of software application development, projects have had three critical business drivers: better cost and schedule management, cycle time improvement, and better quality management. And usually a failure in one realm is considered a project failure. This leads one to wonder what the state of IT projects is in terms of the success or failure rate, in this age of software maturity, in an industry that is more than a decade old. As numerous industry surveys and empirical data have shown, the top reasons found for project failures are lack of user input, incomplete requirements and specifications, changing requirements, and lack of executive support. All of this leads to the conclusion that the business value of IT is still only vaguely perceived. And with the current watch on technology investments, there is even greater need for measuring

ROI on technology investments. A disciplined approach to software generation is essential if this goal is to be accomplished.

Quality Has to Reflect on the Bottom Line

When you look at an industry structure, it becomes apparent that the focus of the players depends on the relative competitive positioning. In a monopoly or an oligopoly (few key players), the companies typically look at their cost and add a markup (to get the sought-after market volume) to get to a certain selling price. The equation looks like this:

$$\text{Cost} + \text{Profit} = \text{Selling Price}$$

But as the industry structure moves toward pure competition with many players providing almost a commodity product/service, the perspective of the equation changes. Mathematically, it remains the same:

$$\text{Selling Price} - \text{Cost} = \text{Profit}$$

But it's a whole different paradigm since the players have similarly priced products, because the only way to gain competitive advantage is to focus on minimizing the costs to add to the bottom line (assuming that it's not realistic for the players to engage in a price war for market share expansion). And this is exactly where we find the IT and application development industry. The current critical nature of software and application development in products or service offerings has elevated the importance of the software process in ROI considerations. Especially for any new IT initiative, there is a lot of soul-searching for the return on investment. And as we saw in the previous section, the software failure rate is still high even when it is becoming critical to almost all segments of the global economy. Unfortunately, a high failure rate leads to high cost of poor quality (COPQ)—direct costs of finding and fixing defects and indirect costs like delayed time-to-market, potential loss of market share, and lowered brand loyalty from the customer. This has a direct impact on the bottom line, and hence there is a growing scrutiny on the ROI of IT projects in general. Maintenance costs can be decreased by reducing rework. Overheads decrease with faster cycle time. Implementation costs decrease with higher productivity. The bottom line savings from these reductions in cost achieve optimal project costs.

Figure 30: Reducing Cost of Poor Quality

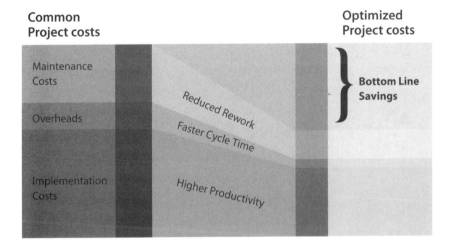

In undertaking any project, it's quite a challenge to summarize the cost and benefit factors and values that contribute to estimating ROI, even with a scholarly analysis of the assumptions surrounding each factor. And this is where Six Sigma offers a set of tools for tracking and enabling success. The Six Sigma value proposition has a phenomenal focus on financial results and hence has the buy-in of top management. This fixation with financial results may sound a bit condescending for a corporate vision or value, but it ensures that executive buy-in remains until the execution and rollout phase

> The ultimate quality award is improved bottom-line profitability.

of a project (the lack of which is a major reason of failure for IT projects). It also ensures business discipline in project selection and project tracking, with a focus on maximizing the benefits delivered to the bottom line. The Six Sigma philosophy is that satisfied customers come back for more and encourage their business associates, family, and friends to do the same. It recognizes that the ultimate quality award is improved bottom-line profitability.

Going back to application development, analysis of many projects has consistently revealed two facts (source—*Juran's Quality Handbook*):

1. Almost half of the development resources are used for testing.
2. Almost 70 percent of total resources over the life of the software are used in maintenance.

Hence, cost savings can be realized only with methodologies that yield high quality initially and manage the change control process. This becomes even more relevant with the recent emphasis on total cost of ownership, which involves a holistic assessment of all the costs (fixed costs—initial acquisition costs, and variable costs—ongoing support costs), including capital investments, license and maintenance fees, direct and indirect labor expenses, training costs, and travel expenses that will be incurred throughout the life cycle of the project. There are essentially two approaches to ensure software quality:

- Assurance of the process by which the product is developed
- Evaluation of the quality of the end product

There is always need to study both the quality of the software product and the life cycle cost incurred in the development and maintenance of the products. The quality of software has been studied mainly from defect analysis and software maintenance perspectives. The effect of the process used in a software project on the outcome of the project in terms of cost to the software developer and quality of the product is key. There are many models that have been used for disciplined application development, and the key to understand is that the disparate quality models need to be evaluated in the context of business objectives. Project characteristics that determine the relevance of a particular methodology can be broadly based on the following dimensions:

- **Project size**

  This is not only the measure of lines of code or megabytes of data, but also—and primarily—the complexity of the system, the nature of its main components, its interactions, and, importantly, the size and composition of the development team.

- **Application domain**

  This includes not only the domain of environmental management but also the characteristics in more technical terms: real-time, distributed (client/server architecture with both LAN and WAN elements), decision support objective, etc.

- **Criticality**

  Projects of high criticality, such as the ones doing forecasting for weather conditions or decision support systems in important domains like emergency health care, need rigorous methodologies to ensure the quality.

- **Innovation**

  If a project is a research project, involving a number of new and not yet proven technologies like 3D dynamic simulation, a fair amount of process customization can be done to eliminate the need to follow rigid procedures.

In their book *Balancing Agility and Discipline*, Barry Boehm and Richard Turner propose an effective technique for evaluating the applicability of certain methodologies for a given project by analyzing the following factors: size, criticality, dynamism, personnel and culture. For example, successful agile projects are likely to have the following characteristics:

- **Size:** The number of people on the project is small, typically less than thirty.
- **Criticality:** The solution is not so important that failure means disaster of one kind or another.
- **Dynamism:** The degree of expected change to requirements is significant.
- **Personnel:** Project personnel tend to be more skilled and able to direct their own work.
- **Culture:** The culture of the organization thrives on change and uncertainty.

Also, as Alistair Coburn mentioned in his book, *Agile Software Development*, the size and complexity of the problem should dictate the "heaviness" of the methodology. The methodology should be designed to support the successful delivery of large, complex projects and may be scaled down for smaller projects. The various approaches used in the industry are:

- *ITIL:* A set of best practices and standards for IT services, maintained and developed by the United Kingdom's Office of Government Commerce.
- *COBIT:* Control objectives for information and related technology—an open standard for good IT security and control practices.
- *MRM/IS:* A fully populated database of best practices and samples for IT shops, taking a business architecture approach to information systems. It has much more coverage than ITIL, but ITIL is richer in the areas it covers.
- *GQIM:* Goals, questions, indicators, measures—an approach to measure customer satisfaction in projects.

It's also worth highlighting that Six Sigma for software (SSS) is not a *software* development process definition—instead it's a general methodology for improving processes and products. It provides a holistic quality objective in product development, combining a programmer's desire for a bug-free piece of software and a user's desire for an easy-to-use application that fulfills a business need. Although a few elements of the SSS toolkit are invoked within other methodologies like the PSP/TSP framework (e.g., regression analysis for development of estimating models), there are many other tools available in Six Sigma for generating good quality software products.

Personal software process/team software process (PSP/TSP) are the Software Engineering Institute's processes to enable teams to develop software products more effectively by dramatically improving product quality, increasing cost and schedule predictability, and reducing development cycle time for software. For instance, *voice of customer* (VOC) and *quality function deployment* (QFD) are useful for developing detailed and prioritized customer requirements (both stated and unstated). More than just sending out survey forms, it involves creating a meaningful customer feedback process. This encourages activities that are aligned with the needs of both internal and external customers. The VOC is captured in a variety of ways: direct interviews, surveys, focus groups, customer specifications, observations, etc. This understanding of the customer needs is then summarized in a matrix or QFD. These tools ensure that the following necessary steps are taken care of:

- Apply the steps for identifying customers in a given business scenario.
- Recognize the benefits of clearly defining customers' requirements.
- Apply the steps for creating a critical-to-quality needs tree in a given business scenario.

- Determine the appropriate Kano Model (a product development and customer satisfaction modeling technique to categorize the features needed in a product or service) category on which to focus customer improvement efforts for a given business scenario.

And this is where SSS comes in—preaching the concept that the process of generating the product is more important than the product itself. But an IT person will point out right away that application development is not like manufacturing, since process variation can never be eliminated because of these reasons:

- No two modules are alike, and so performance includes an intrinsic degree of variability.
- There is greater variation in human cognitive processes (differences in skills from one developer to another).
- Quality assurance processes work differently for manufactured goods than they work for software. This is because software products need testing only once before being called "acceptable," and it is the same "acceptable" program that is distributed to customers. Thus, unlike a traditional factory where there are many different independently produced units that are each tested, a software factory produces one program.

Then there are numerous charting and calculation techniques that can be used to scrutinize cost, schedule, and quality data (project level and personal level) as a project proceeds. For technical development, there are quantitative methods for risk analysis and concept/design selection.

> The process of generating the product is more important than the product itself.

Once management has driven the business strategy down to projects, one can work on them with the Six Sigma DMAIC approach. This starts with the assumption that all work is a process, and the goal is to improve the process in general. But Six Sigma applications in software also reach beyond the business goal of improving current processes or products and extend to the design of new processes or products. SSS incorporates the DFSS approach to improving the feature/function/cost trade-off in definition and design of the software product. Tools such as KJ analysis, QFD, conjoint analysis, design of experiments (DOE), and many others have high-leverage applications in the world of new product development in software.

In the software world, it would also heavily leverage reuse libraries that consist of robustly designed software. Heuristically, it has been found in the application development industry that Six Sigma for Software begins to be cost-effective once the organization has reached CMM levels of 4 or 5. As an organization matures to CMM Level 4/5, it begins to truly leverage established measurement practices, and that's when accomplishment of true "six sigma" performance becomes a relevant goal. And at that point, Six Sigma and approaches such as CMM/(I), PSP, and TSP become complementary and mutually supportive. From a corporate strategy viewpoint, Six Sigma is an enabler to launch CMM, CMMI, PSP, etc. with similar tools, methods, and concepts of continuous improvement. And yet it differs from CMM/CMMI in that:

- Six Sigma speaks the *language of business*, addressing costs, profitability, and ROI.
- In Six Sigma, projects are drawn from a portfolio of problems that are identified through *business strategy* while CMM linkage to strategy is weak.
- Six Sigma teams consist of highly trained employees from many departments of the company, not just quality assurance (QA) (called *boundary-less collaboration*).
- An additional distinction is that Six Sigma is typically applied to selected projects, while CMM/I/PSP/TSP are intended for all projects across the organization.

- With conventional practices like CMM, it is easy to fall into the trap of laying a veneer of process over the same old activities.
- The primary goals of CMMI/PSP/TSP are continuous improvement in the performance of software development teams in terms of software product cost, cycle time, and delivered quality. SSS may be applied to achieve many other business objectives as well, such as improved customer service after delivery of the software, improved customer satisfaction, and value realization from the software product feature set delivered. SSS applies to the software process, the software product, and to balancing the *voice of the customer* and the *voice of the business* (a term used to describe the stated and unstated needs of the businesses and shareholders) to maximize overall business value resulting from processes and products.

The most fundamental tenet of Six Sigma is that we must "manage by fact." This view is consistent with that of TSP/PSP, but it has not yet been established that PSP/TSP is the "best" alternative in every context, only that it is better than some alternatives. SSS can help organizations find the solution(s) that is truly optimal for each unique circumstance.

As IT becomes more involved as a business value driver across different industries, there will be improvements in IT's own business processes. This will necessitate IT to become part of strategic processes and use Six Sigma concepts like business initiative evaluation, prioritization and approval, IT resource supply-and-demand balancing process, etc.

> The most fundamental tenet of Six Sigma is that we must "manage by fact."

FIVE

Get Healthy and Stay Healthy

Out of clutter, find simplicity. From discord, find harmony.
In the middle of difficulty, lies opportunity.
—Albert Einstein

It is widely understood that if a person eats right and exercises then he or she can lose a desired amount of redundant weight and be healthy. But in many cases if the person returns to the same habits of unhealthy eating and lack of exercise, then the unwanted weight will return. A recent study by researchers at the University of Missouri (as described by the website Science Daily) takes it a step further. What they found is that even with regular physical exercise, people who are otherwise sedentary are at higher risk for chronic diseases such as diabetes, obesity, and liver disease. They found that it is not enough to exercise regularly if a person otherwise sits in one place for most of the day. Likewise, keeping IT operations healthy requires more than occasional bursts of helpful activity to rationalize and standardize. It is an ongoing activity to be re-examined as part of a regular exercise like annual planning. Business–IT alignment and integration require that both parties take stock of the current situation, consider in what ways they wish to improve, and then determine how to get there.

Many CIOs are looking at optimizing their IT asset portfolio, and the questions they are asking are: "How can I reduce costs and inefficiencies in my IT operations? How can I improve application performance? How can I reduce complexity within the IT environment? And lastly, if I am able to achieve the above mentioned, how can I ensure that the chaos in the IT asset portfolio, once under control, does not return?"

> Ensure that the chaos in the IT asset portfolio, once under control, does not return.

There are different "physics" that get the firm to this hairball of applications and infrastructure—governance and funding mechanisms, organization structure, changes in capabilities, leadership gaps, etc. The way to start looking at rationalization is as below. This diagram depicts a number of key points and elements. It outlines the IT drivers (business units, users, and applications) that result in related IT costs (CPU, server, storage, data center, and employees). It indicates that the further to the left changes are implemented (i.e., the drivers), the more positive the impact on the IT costs. Certainly issues along the chain need to be addressed (via the envisaged initiatives), and these will have a positive impact on costs, but the impact will be lessened if not undertaken in conjunction with changes to the IT drivers.

Figure 31: IT Costs Added Up at Every Level of an Organization Function

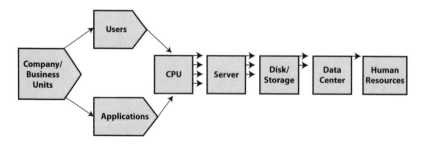

The previous diagram illustrates just how the "chain" impacts the expensive costs due to unbridled growth in IT assets:

- *Company/business units*—In many organizations there is no cross-bank view of TCO, for technology services have led to the proliferation of hardware and software across the IT estate. This leads to higher than usual license costs due to fragmented infrastructure (e.g., SUN, HP).

- *Applications*—Infrastructure is dictated by the growth in the application areas, therefore making efficiency and improvement difficult. Many applications in the company are not maximizing the available server capacity (CPU capacity), yet server hardware specifications are rising.

- *Server*—Distributed computing has led to unchecked proliferation of under-utilized servers (only 10 to 20 percent of CPU capacity actually used), and multiple systems often reside in different places and have different interfaces.

- *Storage*—Storage growth due to growth of the application footprint has kept up with lowered costs in that area.

- *Data center*—There has been a lot of growth in the data center footprint as a result of an increase in server and storage requirements, driven by application development and support.

- *Human resources*—The lack of automation requires manual interaction for servers and applications to support infrastructure globally (e.g., provisioning, backup, etc.). And the need to maintain a wide variety of skills to manage different technologies leads to increased costs.

Several key market drivers are fueling the need for organizations to consider IT assets consolidation:

- *Proliferation of servers*—Because of a lack of standardization in enterprise architecture disciplines, applications are installed on separate servers, as each application requires different server hardware configurations.

- *Increasing storage demands*—Most data centers are populated with servers that have individually dedicated storage systems, and enterprises suffer costly inefficiencies in data storage management.
- *Declining bandwidth costs*—New technologies are decreasing the cost of network bandwidth (e.g., IP VPN, DWDM). Carrier services are at rock-bottom prices, and prolonged price wars are benefiting consumers.
- *Demands to centralize infrastructure, management, and operations*—In order to provide the business with appropriate service levels, there is increasing demand for improved management and control over infrastructure, IT operations, and IT management.
- *Demands to lower total cost of ownership*—Executives who have some familiarity with IT are asking for reduction in hardware and software costs and reduction of operations and management support costs. A recent survey of IT operations spend found that the server capital cost is only a small portion of the overall cost of ownership associated with a server, while nearly 90 percent of the costs lie in management, support, and other ancillary expenses.

Like Nathan Myhrvold said in *Scientific American*, "Software is a gas. It expands to fill its container. . . . After all, if we hadn't brought your processor to its knees, why else would you get a new one?"

What to Rationalize

So even before we answer any IT value targeting questions to consider IT asset rationalization, it is important to list out the typical IT assets, since this helps create the right context for assessing opportunities for consolidation. Depending upon the industry that a company is in, these IT assets can be broadly categorized into the following two groups:

1. *Infrastructure:* Typical infrastructure consists of desktops, laptops, printers, servers, PDAs, voice communication (PBXs, handsets, cell phones, pagers, etc.), data communication (bridges, routers, hubs, multiplexers, firewalls, circuits, modems, etc.), storage (tape drives, direct access storage device [DASD] used for mainframe storage, storage area network [SAN], network-attached storage [NAS], etc.) and facilities.

2. *Applications/Software:* Typical applications or software consist of packaged software, custom software, operating systems, middleware, databases, etc.

With the broad range of IT assets that generally exist, strategic decisions typically need to be made as to what to consolidate and rationalize. Moreover, it has typically been seen that these initiatives should always be done in concert with business counterparts in the organization. Especially as one moves from infrastructure (plumbing) to the application side of the house, business partnership brings the much-needed ROI, since its buy-in is critical to achieve potential benefits.

> These initiatives should always be done in concert with business counterparts in the organization.

Some of the empirical data shows that if you categorize various infrastructure asset rationalization efforts into value delivered versus cost and effort, the best consolidation targets are as follows:

Figure 32: IT Consolidation Options

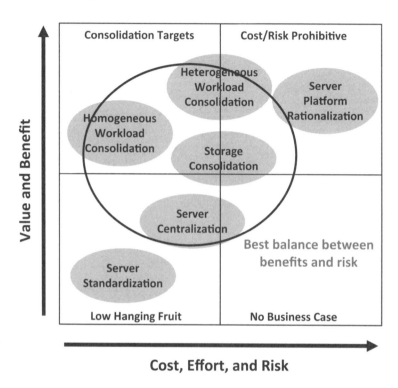

An integrated approach should examine seven interrelated domains and identified actionable initiatives. The IT asset optimization project should be confined to high-level infrastructure and application analysis. All other focus areas need to be evaluated relative to their relationship with application and infrastructure optimization goals.

Infrastructure Rationalization

It is amazing to see how the evolution of the CIO function has taken place over the years. Many senior IT executives who had their grounding in the infrastructure side of the IT organization, specifically data centers, rose high in the company because data centers were capital intensive assets and managing those involved the whole IT organization. Such folks when promoted to the CIO level were very good at understanding the IT operations and how to keep the lights on with the right level of operational efficiency. This was their bread and butter, and they did this pretty well. But some of them had challenges when they sat down with their business counterparts to define and operationalize the company strategies. They had a tough time in being the business partners because they did not speak that language. That's why in recent times one sees more folks on the application development and management side rise up to senior leadership levels in the IT organization. With their groundings ranging from front-end revenue generating CRM systems to the back-office ERP systems, they always had to sit down with their business folks and can partake in the value-targeting strategies.

Nevertheless, whichever route the IT leader ascends from, his or her three main functions remain the same—taking on the right amount of projects (being effective), putting in the right methodology to get the needed applications/systems going, and lastly, managing the technology infrastructure efficiently.

There are many levers that involve consolidating the infrastructure:

- *Server consolidation*: Consolidating multiple applications on one server reduces server sprawl and enables better management and utilization of computing resources.
- *Storage consolidation*: The sharing of centralized storage by multiple heterogeneous hosts. Combining server and application consolidation with centralized storage makes data more easily available to many applications, and this can be achieved through use of SAN/NAS technologies to allow storage to be shared across multiple servers.
- *Middleware*: Customers using multiple directory services can consolidate and simplify their directory services by

standardizing on a single directory product that uses open standards, such as lightweight directory access protocol (LDAP), and scales to encompass the entire enterprise.

- *Desktops*: By consolidating applications and data centrally, you can provide a secure, massively scalable environment for your business, offering the freedom to use any device end users choose, while protecting your company's resources.
- *Processes*: Procurement, provisioning, and support.
- *Server platform rationalization*: Consolidation of multiple platform "flavors" into one or few.

Data Center Consolidation

Today's global organizations are inherently complex, and nowhere is this fact more evident than in a company's data center. The scene is often chaotic: data centers with hundreds (if not thousands) of servers and storage units, multiple databases and dozens of operating systems—all needing to work together seamlessly to satisfy 24/7 user demands and business process application requirements.

Over the years, a proliferation of data centers has occurred largely due to mergers and acquisitions and the historical lack of bandwidth to support performance requirements. Many organizations are now faced with a large number of decentralized data centers in numerous locations with a varying number of servers. Many have multiple data centers and server rooms with less than five servers in each. All of this results in the unnecessary cost associated with administration, maintenance, and depreciation. One of the CIOs I was chatting with mentioned,

> No C-level executive wants to invest in their company's data center, especially not now when the economy is executing an almost perfect swan dive into an Olympic-sized recessionary

pool. But an adequately functioning data center is not a luxury; it's a business necessity. But we have to make sure the redundancies are removed and optimization is practiced in these capex heavy assets.

Reducing cost and complexity by improving performance in the data center is critical for today's organization. Companies can typically achieve a 10 to 30 percent reduction in server TCO by centralizing, consolidating, and standardizing existing servers. The number of servers can often be reduced by 30 to 60 percent. And with the improvement of bandwidth performance, it's advisable for organizations to review their data center footprint and consider a more centralized approach. By conducting a data center assessment, organizations can better understand how many data centers they have, whether they are large, medium, or small operations, what the utilization rates are, and the associated costs involved.

In order to make the data center ready for the future, operations management will still retain focus on core disciplines—system performance management, event/fault management, problem management, operation level management, service level management, and security management. But virtualization of infrastructure requires the approach to IT infrastructure management to become predictive. This involves the extension of infrastructure to the Internet, high availability planning, predictive capacity planning, workload management, etc.

> The company needs to assess its applications and classify them into categories, depending on criticality and availability requirements.

Data Center Migrations Should Be Tier-Centric

The company needs to assess its applications and classify them into categories, depending on criticality and availability requirements. If a company currently has applications categorized in two tiers, each tier will have a different migration method because of the required availability of that tier. Tier 1 could have the critical applications that require high availability. Applications in this tier may include mainframe, key infrastructure components, and critical distributed (e.g., .com). Business continuity and disaster recovery (BC/DR) capabilities of this tier may be mature, but not all applications have a redundant pair. Tier 2 could have the less critical applications. Applications in this tier include backend systems that are used by the company but are not critical to the day-to-day activities. The migration methods used for Tier 1 levels are predominately *lift and shift, clone,* and *rebuild,* as explained below.

Lift and Shift

Pack, load, and move existing hardware and data to the new DC facility. The following explains the rationale and assumptions used in industry leading to the selection of a *lift and shift* migration strategy:

- Servers that are not critical for daily business operation are prime candidates for this strategy.
- Extended downtime is acceptable or low risk.
- Application is very hardware specific.
- Hardware refresh is not planned and existing hardware must be reused.
- High risk servers where migration could have a major impact to system stability/availability should also be migrated using this method.
- Documentation and clear understanding of the application/infrastructure device that resides on the server is not available.
- High volume of data resides on the server and must be available in its entirety to keep the application/infrastructure device stable.

Clone

Acquire and install compatible equipment to receive logical data and processes. The following explains the rationale and assumptions used in an industry leading to the selection of a *clone* migration strategy:

- Server downtime is not an option.
- High risk servers where migration could have a major impact to system stability/availability.
- Documentation and clear understanding of the application/infrastructure device that resides on the server is not available.
- High volume of data resides on the server and must be available in its entirety to keep the application/infrastructure device stable.
- Technology refresh is in scope.
- This option is generally used for custom business applications.

Rebuild

Acquire and install compatible equipment, OS, and applications and reconfigure to receive data and processes. The following explains the rationale and assumptions used in the industry leading to the selection of a *rebuild* migration strategy:

- Application/infrastructure device is selected for hardware refresh/upgrade.
- Application must be reinstalled and reconfigured on refresh hardware in order to function.
- Business application and infrastructure devices requirements/interdependencies dictate minimal server downtime
- Documentation and support is fully available.

The migration methods for this Tier 2 level (not as critical applications) are predominately *P2V* and *swing* as explained below:

Physical to Virtual (P2V)

Take a standard physical device and generate a new virtual machine automatically based on the physical device's configurations and settings. This is to free up the source equipment to be returned to vendor, reused, or retired. Custom business applications will generally not fall under this category because of a lack of virtualization support, resource/time requirement, and high risk. The following explains the rationale and assumptions used in the industry leading to the selection of a *P2V* migration strategy:

- Business critical systems require 100 percent up time.
- They do not have a database and are not highly I/O intensive. Generally low I/O intensive infrastructure devices such as application portal servers using active directory (AD) may be virtualized. Standard devices such as Citrix and AD are fully supported by virtualization platforms.

Swing

Acquire and install a subset of compatible equipment to receive logical data and processes. Utilize freed up hardware from post migration, disconnect source equipment, and ship to the location for the next phase of relocation. The following explains the rationale and assumptions used in the industry leading to the selection of a *swing* migration strategy:

- Used for mission critical and highly complex application server/infrastructure devices where virtualization is not supported.
- Used when downtime is not an option and the migration needs to be done in a phased approach.
- This approach is recommended for AD based applications where domain name/server name must be kept constant.

Benefits for Data Center Consolidation

1. **Cost reduction**—Consolidation leads to a reduced number of locations, which helps with facilities costs—power, HVAC, rent, security, etc. It also leads to increased economies of scale for location-intensive activities like physical management, systems monitoring, etc. This economy of scale helps in reducing IT procurement costs. Also, the business continuity and disaster recovery plans can be re-tiered to optimize SLAs, which could lead to a reduction in service costs.

2. **Cost elimination**—This helps in the reduction of the server footprint and contains unnecessary processor growth via improved processor utilization. The reduced capital and depreciation charges for this and the reduced network connections/lines are some other benefits that can be accrued.

3. **Operational efficiency**—Once the data centers are consolidated and optimized, companies have seen dramatic improvements in data center operations like streamlined deployment of new servers, storage, etc. The higher and standardized data center standards increase service resilience and availability (leading to reduced downtime costs). These harmonized operations provide a greater capacity for scalable growth and better utilization of highly skilled personnel.

4. **Risk mitigation**—Harmonized operations mitigate business risk by having appropriate mission critical facilities, improved disaster recovery, improved business continuity planning, etc.

5. **Capability improvement**—These consolidated and optimized data centers enable faster time-to-market for business-critical applications, modularize services to businesses at various levels (e.g., storage, computing, databases, etc.), and lead to improved asset transparency.

Application Rationalization

Despite your application rationalization efforts, you will still have an average of 4-7 percent CAGR in your application portfolio.
—Gartner 2009, an industry publication

Some organizations waste significant portions of their IT budget on redundant, under-performing, complex applications. For many companies, a majority of IS and IT budgets are allocated to application maintenance and support, even up to as much as 80 percent. Not only does this decrease profitability, but it also reduces available capital for discretionary spending and strategic initiatives. Repositioning this spending is a critical lever for an effective IT organization. Several major factors have contributed to an increased focus on simplifying the application portfolio through rationalization and improved portfolio management:

> For many companies, a majority of IS and IT budgets are allocated to application maintenance and support, even up to as much as 80 percent.

- Many years of distributed IS/IT spending and investment within specific functions and/or organization boundaries (no enterprise-wide investment management process)
- Increased cost pressure and desire to improve the synergy of IS/IT investments across organization boundaries (eliminate redundant vendor/technology investments, consolidate IT assets)
- Growing need to integrate infrastructure and enterprise solutions across external customers, suppliers, and partners
- Significant merger/integration activity to achieve economies of scale and remain competitive

- Growing demands from the business to increase the strategic utilization of information technology and produce greater impact from the existing levels of IS/IT investment

As per Forrester Research ("Building the Business Case for APM"—October 20, 2005),

> In the late 1990s, CIOs avoided investments in legacy systems because the mainframe was being replaced. In 2000, the recent Y2K investments made migration unthinkable. In the early 2000s, the Internet craze kept our attention elsewhere. In 2005, most companies are finally admitting that their legacy environments will be with them for a decade or more. So Application Portfolio Management (APM) will help make sense of the chaos that plagues most IT organizations. This is as true for five-year-old C, C++, and VB environments as it is for thirty-year-old mainframe COBOL environments.

Application rationalization is a systematic approach to improving the business performance of IT application portfolios by reducing current system complexity and by aligning application direction to the priorities of the business. By eliminating redundant applications, retiring end-of-life applications, and renewing high-value applications running on outdated platforms, companies can decrease their application and infrastructure expenses. They can also shift existing application maintenance spending to strategic investments. Also, business integration costs decrease and clients report increased business flexibility from fewer applications. And to achieve maximum results, application rationalization efforts must start with a clear understanding of current and future business priorities. Applying business prioritization criteria to the current application portfolio enables reallocation of IT resources to the highest value areas. Adopting standard platforms (and striving to attain a smaller systems footprint), employing vanilla applications, and reducing the number of legacy systems enables an organization to not only reduce and/or redefine its maintenance/investment mix, but also reduce the hardware footprint (e.g., number of servers necessary to host applications, etc.). This reduction in hardware and infrastructure costs frees up additional funds for strategic investment or lower overall operating costs.

Application rationalization is most successful when completed in conjunction with an effort to change the structures, processes, and organization disciplines that manage and control IS/IT spending. The company can have separate efforts underway evaluating the IS/IT operating model and governance direction. These efforts are complementary to application rationalization activities and should be pursued in parallel to the application rationalization activities.

- *Application rationalization:* The usual *inventory–analyze–justify–rationalize* cycle of business systems (as first introduced by AMR—"A Four-Step Process to Application Rationalization," June 24, 2003). Have an inventory of your applications—this is the starting point. There are homogeneous workload consolidations, where the integration of similar applications on servers and storage systems that support different types of workloads are consolidated. There is also heterogeneous workload consolidation, where the integration of different applications on systems that support different server types, operating systems, and applications replace multiple systems.

- *Operating environment:* This is about reducing the number of OS (operating systems) platforms to support, which reduces complexity, reduces staffing requirements, and enables IT to refocus on business goals.

To attain significant cost savings and realignment of investment spending requires a strategic intervention in how applications are managed and maintained. The right approach to application rationalization should involve a disciplined methodology for evaluating and managing applications as a portfolio. For this, each major application or application family should be evaluated based on its functional and technical adequacy to meet the business need. The typical scope of application rationalization develops an enterprise-wide view of the targeted strategic systems, across organizations, functions, and programs, while simultaneously categorizing all non-strategic applications into one of several future disposition classes.

If the underlying causes of application redundancy and complexity are not understood and removed, the organization may not accomplish the rationalization goals and will migrate back to its original state. Establish governance and clear accountabilities to ensure that the process is disciplined and sustained. Allocate sufficient resources to support the process and develop an objective prioritization framework. Also, throughout the effort it is important to maintain communication and education programs—as explained earlier in this book, a change enablement effort, needs to run concurrently depending on the scope and impact of change.

The business is greatly impacted by such an effort; without its members' participation and understanding of "what is in it for them," the effort will be limited or completely unsuccessful. Application rationalization is first and foremost a business activity. Typically application rationalization is undertaken as part of an organization-wide effort to reduce spend—not just IT spend. High-level sponsorship is required to generate and maintain the sense of urgency around the rationalization effort. It is very important to link the effort with business simplification and cost take-out. Therefore, process and organiza-

> Process and organizational streamlining in conjunction with application rationalization is generally the key to success.

tional streamlining in conjunction with application rationalization is generally the key to success. One of the SVPs involved in helping with application rationalization strategy said,

> Bringing in some stakeholders who represent the users of the application and the technology folks who build and maintain those applications and letting them have a true conversation was effective. Instead of a lecture or a diatribe, we let the conversations flow, and then the impact of the entire organization came to the fore and what that journey might entail began to get clear.

In most companies, the business units typically use the excuse that they need their own applications because they have a very unique process or capability. An experienced data collection team interviewing the business units together and discussing the process flows can help with this problem. When the business units are in the same room to discuss their "unique" processes, often they quickly realize they were not that unique after all.

Involve the financial department of the company. The overall value case created for the project should be kept fresh as project business cases are developed and completed to demonstrate success and maintain momentum.

Much of what you can do in your application rationalization and cost optimization efforts is a function of how mature the company's enterprise architecture is. A strong enterprise architecture is the foundation for execution in such initiatives. Many of the benefits from a simplified application and technology portfolio come from increased information reliability and availability, higher interoperability, and extended business relationships through a more effective services/integration architecture. The company needs to develop an architectural vision for the information and integration layers and create an architects' toolbox to drive toward a simplified technology architecture.

Infrastructure and other IT areas are typically rationalized and consolidated prior to engaging the business in application rationalization. However, as the application portfolio is reduced, further infrastructure consolidation is usually possible. The key is to understand both the functional and technical rationale (at all architecture layers) for classifying an application as strategic, consolidation target, sunset, and elimination. It is important to keep the entire strategic set of applications in mind to drive toward the most homogenous enterprise technology environment. After the initial rationalization decisions have been made, account for the infrastructure. Make sure that you have not selected an application that requires a rogue platform to be maintained (e.g., one remaining application requires the continued support and maintenance of the mainframe system).

> It is important to keep the entire strategic set of applications in mind to drive toward the most homogenous enterprise technology environment.

An Approach for Application Rationalization

1. Launch application rationalization initiative.

The goal of the first step is to understand the company's strategic direction with the business strategy established and approved. The steps involved are as follows:

1. Project initiation/mobilization.
2. Identify both the functional and technical application stewards and owners.
3. Conduct interview sessions with key stakeholders as to the need of the applications and the interdependencies on other business units' applications.
4. Liaise with business stakeholders to determine current strategies and growth areas. Identify weighting criteria from the business perspective.

261

5. Liaise with IT organization stakeholders to identify current strategies and growth areas and pain points. Identify weighting criteria from the IT organization's perspective.
6. Finalize scope—depth, breadth, coverage—of all the applications involved.
7. Confirm this application inventory.

By the end of this step, all applications should be identified and inventoried. The goal should also be to map the infrastructure that these applications sit on. The application scoring method and participants should be identified and availability confirmed. One caveat in this initial step itself is that you should stop using the term "the business." Use "stakeholders" instead. You have to think of your applications and process like a "supply chain." You have demand-side stakeholders (i.e., business organizations, executive sponsors, committees, regulatory bodies/organizations, federal/state/local agencies, trading partners, affiliates, subsidiaries, etc.). And then you have supply-side stakeholders (i.e., anyone who produces, supports, or delivers applications or related services).

Another important note at this stage is that overall governance is needed for such an initiative. This is a part of application portfolio management, and this is simply a part of that enterprise and corporate governance, and application rationalization is part of portfolio management. Every application rationalization effort should have a named owner, usually an executive sponsor or leader. The business stakeholders should always meet with the IT and enterprise architecture groups present.

2. Diagnose the application portfolio.

Now that you have an inventory of the applications, the team needs to map applications to business processes. It needs to conduct the following activities:

1. Determine application health (technical and functional) and strategic alignment.
2. Conduct financial analysis using models like total cost of ownership, which incorporates the allocated/direct maintenance costs for these applications.
3. Conduct follow-up interviews as required.
4. Identify top applications by cost and support full-time employees (FTEs).

It helps to create a heat map that shows the application groups supporting each piece of the value chain—channels, functions, transaction processing, information sources, and back office systems. The application groups are typically then color coded as good, manageable, or inadequate. This visual representation and summary of problem areas establishes the need for further investigation in those areas. The number of applications within each group can be labeled to show the scale of rationalization that might be needed.

Many times the tendency of such initiatives and their sponsors is to try and rationalize all applications. Instead, the initiative should focus the effort on the applications that potentially provide the biggest value once rationalized. For the applications in your portfolio, you should measure:

- *Cost*—Involve the finance department. "We can't determine the cost" is unacceptable. The team will have to use some allocation mechanisms to build the right business case, as explained in the earlier chapters. And even with the cost focus, you need to focus on the predictable technology life-cycle events, such as upgrades, replatforming, etc.
- *Utilization*—The team needs to determine how and how much the application is being used. You can count business transactions and related metrics but not necessarily log-ons, since that does not guarantee activity. Trend this data to try to gauge the value of the application.

- *Risk*—As always you have to gauge the business, technology, and vendor risk.

3. Dispose applications and confirm opportunities.

Next, major applications that meet adequacy criteria are assigned into major classification areas or types based on a set of key prioritization criteria. Typically, five to six major application rationalization categories are defined based on the unique needs of the client's business and technical environment. The following figure illustrates typical application disposition categories and resulting investment management behavior.

Figure 33: Application Disposition Matrix

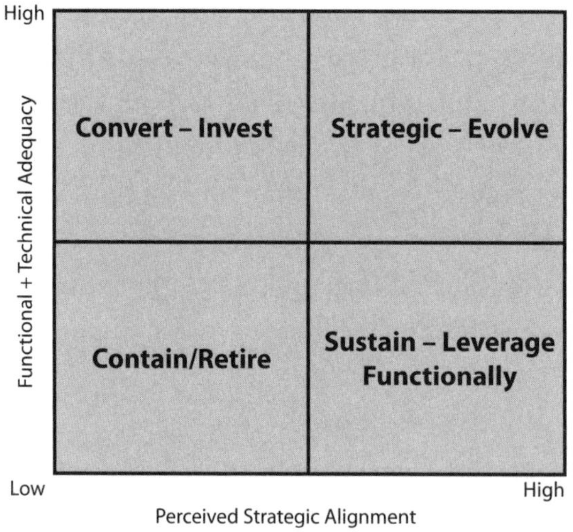

- If the strategic alignment is low and the functional and technical adequacy is low, these applications are good candidates for retirement and migration.
- If the strategic alignment is low but the application has high functional and technical adequacy to its place in the value chain, these applications are good candidates for investment and conversion to strategic uses.

- If the strategic alignment is high and the functional and technical adequacy is low, these applications need to be sustained because they are still important.
- If the strategic alignment is high and the functional and technical adequacy is also high, these applications need to evolve into better usage so they create competitive advantage for the company.

The key in the above diagram is the perceived strategic alignment plotted on the x axis. This category is company-specific (based on business objectives). For this example, it can be based on criteria like alignment with the strategic technology standards, corporate objectives (market position, competitive advantage, customer satisfaction, etc.), or business criticality.

An example application rationalization classification scheme is below:

Classification	Characteristics	Policy
Strategic	• Best positioned to meet current and future business requirements	• Encourage new investment in such applications • Support and promote these applications as strategic
Convert Application	• Application redundant to a similar strategic application • User group/process requires active application support	• Convert the application functionality and information assets within to the "strategic" category

Classification	Characteristics	Policy
Migrate Data	• Functionality exists in another, more strategic, application • Capability no longer requires active maintenance of application functionality	• Migrate only information to the target system and then retire the legacy application(s)
Sunset and Sustain	• Unclear or decreasing value/impact • Cost of migrating or converting exceeds the gain/value of taking action	• Provide break/fix supporwvwt for these applications and allow no new enhancements/functionality unless required to reach a specific strategic goal
Retire	• No clear business reason to sustain the application or the information • Value of eliminating the application outweighs the cost of leaving/supporting	• Eliminate the application and data

The team now needs to analyze the application scores and identify initial application disposition. It needs to justify scores against the initial hypothesis and institutional knowledge and determine quick wins for the conversions, migrations, etc. It needs to validate the scoring across applications and within each logical unit (lines of businesses, domains, etc.).

4. Blueprint future state.

Now the team needs to start analyzing these applications based on the enterprise architecture standards and provide recommendations. It needs to structure simplification recommendations for the current application environment. It needs to map the application against the future state solutions and finalize short-term and long-term strategies. Usually the teams are requested to determine the high-level benefit/cost of disposition to generate a pain/gain matrix. A feasibility analysis needs to be done to see both *pains* (challenges) and the *gains* (benefits) associated with optimization strategies to help formulate the to-be blueprint.

> A feasibility analysis needs to be done to see both **pains** (challenges) and the **gains** (benefits) associated with optimization strategies to help formulate the to-be blueprint.

Complexity, implementation risk, project duration, and project size are all constraints and pain factors. Resolving them, however, allows the gains of cost reduction, operational efficiency, capability improvement, and risk mitigation. The pain versus gain balance provides an approach to decide the future state.

5. Create Road Map.

*It's much easier to point out the perils
of the gap than to contribute to building the bridge.*
—Chris Brogan, marketing consultant and author of *Trust Agents*

The application renewal strategies need to be grouped into logical programs. The team needs to identify organizational and process impacts and create near-term and long-term road maps. Like with any other initiative, the team needs to identify a *benefits realization* method so that the business case progress can be managed. To keep the momentum of the program, the team needs to initiate quick hit opportunities and also explore how road map initiatives fit into the current backlog of projects. Application rationalization initiatives should be treated like a program—they require the proper attention, training, budget, communication, staffing and skills, and partners.

> Identify a *benefits realization* method so that the business case progress can be managed.

Figure 34: Understanding the Gaps and Creating Adequate Road Map

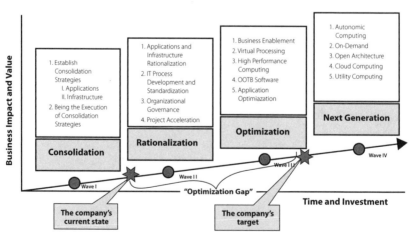

Afterword

What I have tried to do all through this book is offer a framework of how to think of *what* your business does or should be doing and what IT and systems should be doing, *how* they should be doing that, and optimizing what you have in terms of assets for all of the above. The high-level summary of all you read is that there are three components to define your strategy—doing the right things, doing those correctly, and maintaining the health of your business asset portfolio.

As someone said, "A framework is an understanding of how something works and how the component parts of the system work together." The framework you have studied in this book helps establish the interrelations among the multitude of IT components. By continuing to explore a systems view of such solutions, you will ensure that:

- Your business has a framework for considering the recommended capabilities you should focus on building.
- Everyone involved shares a language for discussing and describing what needs to be accomplished and how to build it.

- All aspects of each element are considered, such as the values and beliefs of the organization, measures of desired performance, control of them as the solution is being operated, interfaces with other systems, and the future state of the capabilities needed.
- The basis for continued learning and change is established.

As you and your company move forward in 2012 and beyond, building new capabilities based on the IT framework you have established, strive to maintain the following shifts in your thoughts and actions:

- From "If it ain't broke, don't fix it" to "How do you know it ain't broke if you don't look at it in a different way?"
- From "Work on the right problem" to "Achieve the right purposes."
- From "People resist change" to "People accept change when they are asked the right questions in helping to develop it."
- From "It's not in the budget" to "How could we change it so it makes sense financially?"
- From "Management won't buy it" to "What would make management excited about doing it by targeting the right value?"

Well, I once again want to thank you for going through this book and genuinely hope you found it useful. If you have any thoughts or stories you would like to share after reading it, I would love to hear from you at mail@ashubhatia.com. May your IT prosper and your business flourish!

About the Author

Ashu Bhatia has significant experience in IT and management consulting in the United States, Europe, and Asia. A certified Six Sigma black belt, he has worked extensively in the areas of business architecture, strategy and transformation, customer relationship management, supply chain management, business intelligence, and lean service operations. With a MBA from Carnegie Mellon University, he is a frequent industry speaker on these topics. He has held management positions with Accenture, Siemens, Ciber, and American Express and currently works for RCG Global Services as the managing principal for its southeast region.

Beyond the Light